From the Shrink's Couch . . .
what is being said about:

the Vocational Shrink

Brian Tracy
Author
The Psychology of Selling
www.BrianTracy.com

"This insightful book shows you how to get the most out of yourself and your colleagues in a fast-moving, competitive business world."

Dr. Joe Vitale
Author, "The Attractor Factor" *and way too many other books to list here* www.mrfire.com

"How do you end the unspoken war between employers and employees? This Book, Game and Seminar is the way to get them started on the same page, avoiding the costly misunderstanding and wasteful 'water cooler' sessions so common in the American workplace. This tool will save you a bundle of money, time, and frustration!"

Jim Cathcart
Author
The Acorn Principle
Lake Sherwood, CA
www.cathcart.com

"All self improvement begins with Self-Awareness. Socrates told us 'Know Thyself' and now John Schaefer shows us how. As the 'Vocational Shrink' John walks you through an entertaining and insightful look at how you and others deal with the workplace. Then he shows you how to free yourself from disillusionment. You are going to enjoy this book!"

Scott Alexander
Author
Rhinoceros Success
(800) 872-3274

"If you are going to have a job, you might as well be good at it. John Schaefer's book will help you succeed at dealing with the number one problem in the workplace – People!"

there's more . . .

Peggy McColl
Author
The 8 Proven Secrets to SMART Success
www.destinies.com

"Where was this guy during my earlier career? This illuminating view through your employee's eyes will certainly open yours AND you will be experiencing a substantial increase in income, bonuses and compensation!!!"

Randy Gilbert
host of "TheInside SuccessShow.com"

"John Schaefer is funny and on point and a God-Send for every Human Resources executive! Get 'The Shrink' into your business, then stand aside as your employees beat a path to lowering your costs and improving your ROI!"

Marilyn Spooner
President & CEO
Meetingoals, Inc.

"I have worked with John Schaefer for almost 20 years on highly personalized recognition pro-grams for some of my largest corporate clients. Having partnered with many vendors over the years, I can say without question that John is one of the most creative, thorough, and profes-sional people I have ever met.

When I saw his new book, *The Vocational Shrink*, my first thought was — who better to bring this message of communication, recog-nition, appreciation and growth to corporate America. John has a natural empathy and understanding for the employee that is genuine and heart-felt.

I am thrilled to be able to recommend his Book, Game and Seminar to any company that truly cares about their workers and wants to enjoy all of the financial and emotional benefits available through a better, more cooperative environment between employees and their supervisors."

Betty Doran, PHR
Director of Human Resources,
Collins College
Tempe, AZ

"A must read. This book is an invaluable resource tool that will help each of us discover things about ourselves, our coworkers and the staff we supervise. The book is written in a straightforward, engaging style and full of 'realistic' examples."

The Vocational Shrink

—

An Analysis of the Ten Levels of Workplace Disillusionment

The
Vocational
Shrink

*An Analysis of the Ten Levels of
Workplace Disillusionment*

by John R. Schaefer
*Illustrations by Brian Freeman
Forward by Jim Cathcart*

*Art Direction and Design by
Patty H. Findley — Turn Key Design, Tucson, Arizona*

Library of Congress Cataloging-in-Publication Data

Schaefer, John R.
    The Vocational Shrink – An Analysis of the Ten Levels of
        Workplace Disillusionment
    ISBN   0-9769986-0-2
    1. Business   2. Employee recognition   3. Employee/Manager relations

©2005, Schaefer Recognition & Media Group,LLC
7131 West Planada Lane
Glendale, Arizona 85310

Printed in the United States of America

Schaefer Recognition & Media Group, LLC
is a division of Recognition Concepts, Inc.

ISBN   0-9769986-0-2

All inquiries for volume purchases of this book should be addressed to Schaefer
Recognition & Media Group LLC, at the above address. Telephone inquires may
be made by calling (888)646-6670 or visiting
www.VocationalShrink.com

To all of my bosses, colleagues, friends
and associates who travel the *Ten Levels* with me
as we all strive for recognition, fulfillment and
growth in our work.

Acknowledgments

This work is the culmination of a series of events, awarenesses, and the creative input of a group of co-workers. Mixed with time, experience and a lifelong appreciation of both the frailty and tenacity of human beings, I have been able to capture some of the good and bad, obvious and subtle, serious and funny, and ultimately, the successful and flawed ways that people survive in the American workplace.

I am forever grateful to and appreciative of:

• My wife Sandy, son Ian, and daughters Rachael and Sarah for consistently being examples of the best characteristics of human beings, and for believing in me as I have pondered what work, family and life are all about.

• Larry, for the time and the deep belly laughs we had as the *Ten Levels* took shape, so many years ago.

• Doug, for his friendship and help in developing my spiritual insights that gave this book a happy ending and let my life take on a whole new level of meaning.

• All of the coworkers, colleagues, and managers from whom, by their struggles, victories, frustrations, and decisions, I was able to draw to make this book both fun to read and meaningful to study.

Contents

Forward

In this thought-provoking book, consultant and author John Schaefer takes a pithy, yet light-hearted look at a very real and serious problem plaguing today's businesses. This problem is one that is growing and promises to be an even bigger challenge in the years ahead. What's the problem? It's the rising level of employee apathy in the workplace.

Many employees today suffer from an emotional lethargy. Their work saps their emotional energy. This in turn causes a drain of mental energy that leaves them surviving rather than thriving in their jobs. Survival causes many to take on reactionary, subconscious habit patterns which Schaefer refers to as the *Ten Levels of Workplace Disillusionment*.

This emotional lethargy and the resulting mental fatigue show up in the loss of hard dollars on the organization's bottom line. It results in lower levels of performance and declining customer satisfaction in an already competitive world marketplace. Cumulative results include higher levels of absenteeism, workman's compensation claims, reduced morale, motivation, productivity, cooperation – the list goes on! All of this ultimately leads to increased employee turnover that costs American business billions of dollars per year in additional recruiting and lost training costs.

Some experts have termed this quality of emotional connection of any employee to their work their "level of emotional engagement." In his book, John Schaefer draws on his 20 years of experience starting as an employee, then working with organizations to address their employee engagement issues. Acting as your personal "Vocational Shrink," John explains the stages of, and reasons for, employee disengagement. With his light-hearted approach, Schaefer encourages each reader to examine their own reactionary choices and levels of engagement to understand why and how we all, over time, seem to lose the natural enthusiasm of the new hire.

As the Greek philosopher said, "Know thyself." Enjoy this interesting trip of self-discovery with the "Vocational Shrink" and see how becoming aware of your habit patterns and those of your employees can be the beginning of a very beneficial journey.

Jim Cathcart

Professional speaker and author of
The Acorn Principle and *Relationship Selling*.
Lake Sherwood, California

Part One
Introduction

Anyone who's ever had a job has probably wondered, "Why do people (including me) react the way they do at work?" After careful deliberation of this puzzling question, I submit to you *The Vocational Shrink – An Analysis of the Ten Levels of Workplace Disillusionment.*

We all expect some frustrations and stresses at work. With more options out there than ever before, how do we keep focused, rather than constantly seeing the grass as greener? Managers, how can you be sure that your best workers are fulfilled and aren't looking around at other opportunities? Recognizing some key signs of defensive behavior is part of the answer to both of these questions. Malcolm Forbes said, "If you have a job without aggravations, you don't have a job." It's when these annoyances cause us to take on reactive, often curious, survival mannerisms that it becomes worthy of concern.

The Ten Levels of Workplace Disillusionment will help you bring your subconscious, negative habit patterns into your conscious mind where you can consider options for change. The *Ten Levels* will allow supervisors to quickly identify the behavior patterns taken on by their employees as they struggle with various forms of company politics and office challenges. This tool will offer a framework to both address and help change counterproductive habit patterns in an amusing, yet compelling way. Over time, this realization and alteration of behaviors will create a workplace environment where employees can flourish and reach their peak levels of performance, while assuring your company's strong base of quality personnel, improved profitability and sustained growth.

What started out as nothing more than a couple of employees making silly assessments of fellow workers' reactions to stress in the workplace has, over 20 years, turned into a *Ten Levels* Book, Game and Seminar. Along the way, it has morphed into numerous forms. When we began to realize that our observations of employee behavior had certain consistencies and patterns, we slowly assembled them into the original *Ten Levels*. At this point, these were nothing more than simple descriptions of unique employee behaviors and characteristics that we found interesting and funny.

The original *Vocational Shrink* was a self-help text designed to assist employees in realizing and coming to grips with their negative, reactionary habit patterns. That led to a more complete evaluation of the *Ten Levels* using fictional characters, each based on groups of real people I had worked with early in my career. I also added the chapter on "Common Trends" to explain some of the reoccurring paths taken through the *Ten Levels* during a career. After sharing the manuscript with friends and family, I expanded it to include some advice on how to break free from the grip of the *Ten Levels*, as well as some of my personal journey to freedom. By then, my concept for this book was fully underway.

As my gift and award business Recognition Concepts (Recognition-Concepts.com) grew and my territory representing The Tharpe Company provided me with a wide range of experiences helping organizations recognize and motivate their employees, the idea of *The Vocational Shrink – The Game* also took shape. Having realized that so much of the way we all act and react at work is habitual and subconscious, I knew that an activity allowing all of the employees in a department to participate in a non-threatening, fun, and eye-opening exercise that brought their habits to light in the form of the *Ten Levels of Workplace Disillusionment* made a lot of sense.

Such a game would need to be introduced and taught to groups of employees for it to be effective. *The Vocational Shrink – The Game* would also have to be embraced by management, so must be introduced to the employees in a way that demonstrates a mutual advantage to the workers and the company; no fear, no ulterior motives, no hype. To fully "wrap" this game into the most dynamic format possible, I next evolved our corporate training programs . . . including *The Vocational Shrink – The Seminar.* The *Ten Levels* grew to become a business tool; a vehicle to open up awareness of counterproductive behaviors, evaluate their sources, deal with their effects, and realize the many benefits of improved productivity, morale and, most importantly return on investment, for participating clients.

> "The greater part of our happiness or misery depends on our dispositions, and not on our circumstances."
>
> – Martha Washington

I experimented with the first few levels writing both an "Employee Perspective" and a "Management Perspective" for each . . . attempting to look at each perspective through the other's eyes. Is it wise for a manager to gain a more complete understanding of the specifics of an employee's thought processes and instinctive reactions that lead to his limitations and level of disillusionment? Will an employee benefit from reading about a manager's possible strategies in dealing with staff personality types and overcoming the disillusionment? My feeling is that the *Ten Levels* will be most effective as a tool for business if engaged in openly and proactively by both managers and employees. If either of them disengage, stand aloof, make excuses or cop-out in terms of honestly looking at themselves, the program will ultimately be less effective.

Encouraging this "level" of staff/management interaction adds a deeper dimension to this book and makes understanding the *Ten Levels* concepts easier, more thorough, and will ultimately lead to better results for both employees and managers. The better each of them understands the *Ten Levels*, the more "The Trends" (Chapters 11 and 12) will make sense. The more they embrace the reality of "The Trends", the more motivated they will be to "Get Off the Merry-Go-Round" (Chapter 14) and go on to share in a workplace that is more exciting, friendly, empowering, productive and profitable. This is the win – win – win situation that all organizations yearn for, but so often find to be elusive.

As you study the *Ten Levels of Workplace Disillusionment* – as an employee, a manager or perhaps both – you will gain the ability to identify symptoms of negative behavior patterns, confront them with confidence, and move beyond them to make your work life more enjoyable. You will be properly equipped to share these insights with your coworkers, so that everyone who chooses to will benefit from the synergy that can take the group higher together than any of you could travel alone.

Life is full of situations that, while serious in themselves, can be better comprehended and openly addressed, if looked at from the humorous side. America's first First Lady, Martha Washington, said, "The greater part of our happiness or misery depends on our dispositions, and not on our circumstances. We carry the seeds of one or the other about with us in our minds wherever we go." A lighthearted, open-minded, positive attitude makes evaluation and growth a much more pleasant, fun and rewarding activity. So here's to the understanding of our occupational oddities. Remember, if your job makes you kind of crazy, you're normal!

Part Two
The Ten Levels
of Workplace Disillusionment

The workplace is an exciting arena filled with every kind of person, attitude, lifestyle and skill level imaginable. In studying them all, from the least-skilled blue collar to the highest-qualified white collar, a variety of habits and recurring patterns appear as they deal with the idiosyncrasies and corporate politics present in the work environment.

One of the most interesting aspects of analyzing their traits is the realization that individuals in all echelons of power practice these survival skills to some extent. While managers may choose different levels and behavioral devices than their subordinates, the constant eye toward performance reviews and future promotions causes them all to scurry into their favorite "levels" for relief and safety. These counterproductive reactions to workplace stress can lead to limited cooperation and selfish, protectionistic attitudes.

Not only did I come to recognize these reactive trends, but also to realize that many of the ways particular individuals behaved were subconscious, habit-driven responses that varied by personality type . . . and were totally below their conscious awareness. Norman Vincent Peale taught, "The secret of life isn't what happens to you, but what you do with what happens to you." In the workplace, what people do with what happens is often a reaction, almost an instinct, based on deeply-seated habits they're unaware are controlling them. I'm not an actual psychologist – just "*The Vocational Shrink*" – but have always been fascinated by the patterns of human performance and workplace interactions.

After years of observation, research and more careful analysis, what started out as a fun and harmless game of identifying and cataloging the unique reactions of fellow employees became the progressive *Ten Levels* list. Moreover, three things became obvious:

1. Employees progressed up the levels over time.

2. Personality type, age and education had the most effect on which levels a person chose and how long they stayed there.

3. All of this was well below their conscious level of thinking. These were habit patterns – reactions – not well-thought-out choices.

These observations about working people and their characteristics have been incorporated into the *Ten Levels of Workplace Disillusionment*. While the identification and classification of these behaviors have had me and colleagues rolling on the floor more than a few times, and demonstrated that the *Ten Levels* have a decidedly humorous, "human" side, we're actually dealing with some very serious issues for both workers and employers. During 16+ years building a career in the employee recognition and motivation business, I've gathered the insights and experiences that have resulted in this book.

Not all employees take on the characteristics described in the *Ten Levels of Workplace Disillusionment*. There are many jobs where people are competent, truly appreciated, and manifest that respect and trust in highly productive, rewarding careers. However, there are still a number of companies where employees are left "on their own" to find their individual way to happiness, motivation and success. The probability of the *Ten Levels* being present, and the magnitude of the symptoms, is directly related to the amount of autocratic management and job stress within a given workplace.

Part of the research for this book was gathered while working for a large manufacturing company as an Industrial Engineer, then later for a family-owned, but internationally known, small business. From these experiences and other evidence, I believe the *Ten Levels* may be more pronounced in a small, privately held company environment. Still, throughout the corporate world, the politics and coat-tailing required to survive at any job where you work for someone else can bring about these reactive and destructive characteristics to varying degrees. This book, by no means, intends to paint a picture of all working people ultimately withering away in a downward spiral of occupational hopelessness. The Shrink's job, rather, is to open up the dark corners and shine a light on the devastating, potentially permanent damage that can be done to both employees, and the companies they work for, if the causes and effects of the *Ten Levels* are not dealt with effectively.

Examining these issues will lead to some of the ways one can counteract and overcome these inefficient and demotivating behaviors, once they are identified. This includes reevaluation and modification of habits, changing attitudes, rethinking beliefs, and accessing available resources. That may sound like a lot to tackle, but as Dr. Gary McKay reminds us, ". . . you can't change the effect past influences had on you once, you can only change the effect they have on you now." The more that management and staff can open the lines of communication regarding the causes and effects of workplace frustration, the sooner they can both begin to make the subtle changes necessary to reduce stress, increase cooperation, and greatly improve productivity and satisfaction. Isn't that the winning combination we are all looking for?

The *Ten Levels of Workplace Disillusionment* introduces a sequence of easy-to-recognize behavior patterns that can be used to identify reactive survival tactics that employees fall into unknowingly. Once you can distinguish the effect, you can then match it up with a cause. When both the cause and effect are open on the table, you are free to operate on the underlying problem, bandage up the wounds, and begin to enjoy the fruits of healing.

Employees can be fully utilized, self actualized and highly productive, while employers can maximize the return on their investment of salaries, benefits and training. Both will be happier, healthier, and will create a better company to share with others. Novelist George Eliot put it this way: "What do we live for if not to make the world less difficult for each other."

While gathering this material, I came across some of the most unusual symptoms you can imagine, and they all represent real people and events. Sure, I had some fun and embellished a few of the identifiable symptoms a little, but not so much as to change the relevance of what we observed. I wanted to offer simple, understandable, often funny, but always real, examples of the natural, instinctive reactions of employees when put in a frustrating, demoralizing or fearful environment. As my observations and scribbled notes began to fall into predictable order and repeatable patterns, the *Ten Levels of Workplace Disillusionment* was born.

Over the past 20 years, having moved from an employee who personally experienced many of the levels, to a Recognition Consultant helping companies improve employee motivation and morale, I have grown and finetuned the *Ten Levels* into a form that I'm confident can help both employees and their managers begin to improve their workplaces. My hope is that the awareness of the *Ten Levels of Workplace Disillusionment,* and the fresh understanding of the many ways they can reduce the effectiveness of a workforce, will help to make life at work more fun, rewarding and profitable. Here are the *Ten Levels* as they stand today. In the chapters that follow we will look at each in detail . . . and even share a laugh or two!

The Ten Levels
of Workplace Disillusionment

Level 1 – Disbelief
That stage where the initial naivety of the new employee gives way to the questions, concerns and confusion of illogical corporate politics.

Level 2 – Nodding and Agreeing
The "don't rock the boat" stage – where the confused and/or spineless congregate to brown nose and avoid the frustration of conflicting policies.

Level 3 – Griping and Complaining
Similar to Level 1 (but now you know it's really true). The level where the motivated achievers reside while attempting to progress and find their place in the organization.

Level 4 – Escape
Similar to Level 2, but using crutches like drugs and/or alcohol to handle the frustration, rather than sacrificing one's integrity by becoming a wimp (although the long-term emotional results may be the same).

Level 5 – Gut Check
Characterized by internal physiological complications, such as back aches, ulcers and other intestinal distress.

Level 6 – Class Clown
Includes over-reaction and other bizarre behaviors, usually to counteract Level 3, or hide Level 5 symptoms.

Level 7 – Apathy
The much-envied level of the aging executive who can see the light of retirement at the end of the tunnel. Apathy can also exist in a younger person who feels overlooked and taken for granted, but this is more rare.

Level 8 – Decline and Surrender
Distinguished by external physiological complications brought on by the failed attempt to maintain Level 7.

Level 9 – Paranoia
Incessant whining and fretting due to burnout and mental decline.

Level 10 – Insanity
The ultimate conclusion to the career of the worker who avoids the stagnation of Levels 2 and 4, works past Level 6, fails to maintain Level 7, and survives Levels 8 and 9.

The Ten Levels

DISBELIEF 1	6 CLASS CLOWN
NODDING & AGREEING 2	7 APATHY
GRIPING & COMPLAINING 3	8 SURRENDER
ESCAPE 4	9 PARANOIA
GUT CHECK 5	10 INSANITY

Chapter 1
Level 1 – Disbelief

Most of us start out a new job with great enthusiasm and high expectations. As company politics and unexpected employee interactions begin to attract our attention, Level 1 symptoms are likely to set in. We quickly become irritated at the glaring inconsistencies we see (and everyone else doesn't seem to notice), but we just can't believe that what we are witnessing is for real.

Level 1 lasts from one week to as long as six months. The average employee, however, moves on to Level 2 in about four to six weeks, due to mental fatigue and subconscious survival instinct.

Level 1 symptoms include:

- Shaking head from side to side
- Sighing, rolling one's eyes or looking upwards
- Questioning others repeatedly about a project
- Saying "I just can't believe it" a lot

So this is Level 1. Welcome to the Real World of Work!

... meet Cindy

Cindy graduated from Northwestern just last May and couldn't wait to take on her new responsibilities in the accounting department with Randaletti Technology, Inc. (RTI). During her first 30 days on the job, she eagerly gathered basic knowledge about the company and learned the names of almost everybody on the 3rd floor of the C-1 building. As a Cum Laude accounting graduate, she had all the knowledge she needed to immediately contribute to the company's bottom line, but blending in wasn't quite as easy as she thought it was going to be.

Fran had handled payroll since 1972 and had a funny way of calculating vacation time. Although Cindy had just aced a class that gave her several new ways to computerize this process and make it easier and more fair for both full- and part-time employees, Fran, for some reason, didn't embrace her suggestions.

Cindy also had trouble getting comfortable with Dan, the CFO. Although he was always friendly and helpful, her education and constant enthusiasm seemed to threaten him. He spent too much time justifying his position and qualifications, she felt, and was unwilling to give her any really juicy assignments that were up to her level of talent and capability. Within 90 days, Cindy was beginning to question (in disbelief) many things about the company. What she had been taught in college did not help her in dealing with the people she had to work with, or the systems that often appeared to be anything but state-of-the-art. She quickly learned that it was not a good idea to go over her boss's head in voicing her concerns. Whenever she did, her boss Fran became agitated and Fran's boss Dan just smiled and told her to work it out within the department. Cindy is a classic Level 1 at this stage of her career.

Employee Perspective

If you're reading this as a true Level 1 (Disbelief), you are at a place where most of us have traveled before. Why? A lot has to do with our educational system. Until you get into a Masters or Doctorate program, most, if not all, of your instructors have little or no actual industry experience. They tend to be scholastic achievers who find their passion in teaching.

There is certainly nothing wrong with that; as a matter of fact, we all have stories about the wonderful teachers who shaped our visions, energized our hopes and made our dreams seem achievable. None of us would be where we are today without these wonderful, caring and dedicated professionals guiding our educational life.

The problem is, they have no knowledge or experience with corporate politics; so even if they wanted to, they can offer us no help in this area. There is also pressure on teachers to cover a defined curriculum each semester. This leads to the goal of imparting knowledge and grading tests, with little time left to consider applications in the real world.

That's why when you graduate from college you go through "commencement", a word that means "to begin". You now have amassed a large amount of disassociated knowledge and possess a written credential. This is your ticket to the real world of work where you can "commence" to learn about all of the stress, politics, frustrations, coat tailing and other adventures that make human relations in the workplace so challenging. Like me, a fascination with this aspect of work life can also lead to the opportunity to not only overcome these challenges for yourself, but also to participate in making them better for yourself and others.

Later, we'll get to how you can move beyond "Disbelief".

Management Perspective

Level 1 (Disbelief) employees are a two-edged sword for you as a supervisor. Their naivety can be burdensome from a productivity and initiative point of view; however, they have not been in the working world long enough to develop deep-seated negative habit patterns, so they can prove to be the easiest to bring into a more cooperative, motivated and team-player environment. As you begin to work with your employees to bring the *Ten Levels* to light in your workplace, it is the Level 1 folks who may be the most willing to get on board. While they don't have the experience and have not yet earned the respect of the department (something that can only come with time), they tend to be the most flexible people to work with when it comes to change and trying new ideas.

Because they are still fresh, green, and open, these Level 1 (Disbelief) employees are usually the most eager to bend, because being involved, accepted and appreciated is very important to them. Use them wisely to build a base of enthusiasm, confidence and excitement in your new *Ten Levels*-based initiatives, as others who are far more entrenched in their chosen levels will prove to be much harder to awaken and get on board.

As a manager you also have the advantage of being able to step back and view the various levels in your department from a distance. You will find a macro view of the *Ten Levels* that reside there will be invaluable as you consider how each employee needs to be coaxed into acknowledging their favorite hiding places. Employees will feed off of each other's newly-acquired awarenesses and can serve to make the transition to a more productive and rewarding environment easier for everyone.

Chapter 2
Level 2 – Nodding and Agreeing

After sufficient frustration, the weary Level 1 participant unwittingly slips into Level 2. The mind shuts down a little, and chooses not to make waves – to just go with the flow for a while. Nodding and agreeing may last from one day to forever – in direct proportion to backbone dimensions. While offering a slight reprieve from the anxiety of Level 1, Level 2 obviously represents a potential downfall to any of us with a desire to achieve something with our lives.

Level 2 symptoms include:

- Difficulty making or maintaining eye contact
- An amazing talent for talking in circles
- Reluctance to accept responsibility
- Slumped shoulders

If you're observant, you can see experienced Level 2's nodding and agreeing about some really illogical things. You and your friends can have hours of fun getting well-entrenched Level 2's to contradict themselves and agree to all kinds of counterproductive proposals. It is pathetic what an experienced Level 2 will do to avoid responsibility and controversy.

Although seemingly harmless, a cornered Level 2 will backstab, lie, and fight to maintain his or her space. Many Level 2's are at their peak of the "Peter Principle"[1] defined level of incompetence and are easily threatened. Companies with over-promoted Level 2's in upper management positions find it difficult to let themselves implement the knowledge of subordinate specialists that could be used to outdistance the competition.

"Reinventing the wheel" and long, drawn-out justifications are common within this type of leadership structure. Underutilization of employees, higher-than-average turnover and, ultimately, more costly health insurance premiums often follow.

. . . say hello to Ray

Ray has been with RTI for 29 years and has seen the company grow from a small subcontract shop to a multi-billion dollar manufacturer of specialty parts for the aircraft and computer industries. He began his career working with Bob Randaletti, the Founder and President of RTI, back in Minneapolis when they both got hired on at 3M right out of college.

Ray used to be the Director of Manufacturing and has an office full of plaques and awards celebrating his

---

1 Dr. Laurence J. Peter's famed Peter Principle states that: "Everyone rises to their level of incompetence". Put another way: Everyone rises to at least one level above that at which they are competent.

achievements. He is now Director of the Composites Group, one of six production lines in the company.

Two years ago, RTI brought in an MBA from a Chicago high-tech firm, as VP of Manufacturing, to bring the company into a fully computerized, numerically controlled machine shop with direct PC control, automatic scheduling, and a networked database linking all production processes.

While Ray has a tremendous amount of experience, a corner office, a first-row covered parking spot, a club membership (with a locker two down from Bob), and a block of company NBA season tickets at his disposal, he has become more and more quiet and complacent recently. He never misses an opportunity to be seen nodding and agreeing with Bob and makes sure that he plays the part of his biggest fan. But Bob is less accessible than he used to be. While always pleasant, he has a lot more managers and vendors to deal with than he did 20 years ago when he and Ray ran everything together.

Ray knows all the tricks about how to stay involved and look essential without taking on any more responsibility than necessary or risk shining a light on his lack of current technical expertise. Unfortunately, Bob is oblivious to the dilemma his friend is facing. There are younger employees with more up-to-date computer manufacturing credentials who the company could put in charge of the Composites Group, but no one is about to recommend that to Bob. His connections to Ray are too well known, and Bob still thinks Ray is really making things happen out there.

As Ray gets closer to retirement, he may be able to casually slide into Level 7 (Apathy) and then ride out his final years. But right now, Ray has to keep Bob on his side and appear to have his finger on the pulse of the corporation as protection from a further demotion within the department. He knows there are more qualified candidates for the new, high-tech manufacturing processes that RTI is moving into rapidly, but as long as Bob has faith in Ray, and he can keep up the look of departmental control, he is pretty safe.

While sometimes embarrassed by his Level 2 status, Ray has too much to lose by letting down the facade. He knows he can't gain the knowledge needed to keep up with the younger engineers with shiny new degrees and a lifetime of computer skills. He is also well aware that he could never change jobs and get anywhere near the salary, title, and perks that he enjoys at RTI. Best to just lay low, enjoy the fruits of his labors, and keep his image going as long as possible.

Employee Perspective

As a Level 2 (Nodding and Agreeing), you are one of two types of people. Most likely you are a new Level 2, fresh out of Level 1 (Disbelief) and just resting for a spell while you process all of the new information you recently gained about life in the Real World of Work.

Good news! You still have many options, such as riding out Level 2 for awhile and using the time to collect and process a few career scenarios from a position of comfort and safety. Soon, you will be compelled to jump back into the game as a virgin Level 3 (Griping and Complaining) – perhaps when an exciting-enough growth opportunity makes itself available.

If you are not coming into Level 2 for the first time, then you may be more like our friend Ray, above, who is using Level 2 to protect his/her position and buy time. While self-preservation is an instinctive behavior, Level 2 is not where you ultimately want your instincts to take you. This is the realm of the weak, who rely on old relationships and calling in favors to sustain themselves.

I know I'm pretty hard on long term Levels 2's, but if you find yourself here, take heart; it is still not too late. Remember, you have the advantage of experience and a better understanding of your company than most others, so you have more options to consider. By becoming part of the new interactive team and helping others identify and change their status within the *Ten Levels*, you too will be inspired and invigorated. Rather than use the past to defend your value, be a part of the new direction and you will rise to the top again.

Management Perspective

Where your Level 1 (Disbelief) employees will be the easiest to get on the team, your longest practicing Level 2 (Nodding and Agreeing) folks may be the toughest. A long-term Level 2 is in denial and probably somewhat unaware of how they are perceived by their fellow employees; especially the younger ones. Because they can be seen as sell-outs, living off of past glory, they are not appealing role models to the younger people.

This is reality, but not an insurmountable problem. If you can get a Level 2 actively involved in your department transformation, they are able to both save face and begin to use their vast experience and latent talents in ways they have not recently considered. You stand to salvage a Level 2 (Nodding and Agreeing) victim from continuing down the slippery slope, while at the same time benefiting from their leadership with some of your younger Level 1 (Disbelief), Level 3 (Griping and Complaining), and even some new Level 4's (Escape), if they haven't progressed too far (see Chapters 4 and 12).

Everyone rises

to at least

one level above

that at which

they are

competent.

— Dr. Laurence J. Peter

DISBELIEF	1	6	CLASS CLOWN
NODDING & AGREEING	2	7	APATHY
GRIPING & COMPLAINING	3	8	SURRENDER
ESCAPE	4	9	PARANOIA
GUT CHECK	5	10	INSANITY

Chapter 3
Level 3 – Griping and Complaining

Ahh, Level 3 . . . by far, the most popular level of the working class. It's like Level 1 (Disbelief) in appearance, but with the important contrast that you know and accept the fact that some of your worst expectations are really occurring all around you.

Sure you could quit, but the money's pretty good and what if you couldn't find another job or the new one is as bad as this one? And what about the stock options, the profit sharing, the insurance, blah, blah, blah . . . This is the notable thought pattern of Level 3, which keeps you frustrated enough to resort to griping and moaning as ventilation therapy. Strong Level 3's are most prevalent in family businesses and other heavily bureaucratic organizations that tend to use overpaying as the only meaningful form of employee recognition.

Most of a company's young, enthusiastic new employees bound quickly past Level 2 (Nodding and Agreeing), only to spend the majority of their career in Level 3 (Griping and Complaining), looking for fulfillment and recognition. Unfortunately, the strongest Level 3's are also the employees who are most likely to leave one day and start their own business, or go to a competitor that better motivates and utilizes its people.

It is remarkably easy to get sucked into the lamentations of your local "gripe groups" or "bitch bunches" around the water cooler or lunchroom to let off a little steam, where you'll hear ". . . so and so did such and such . . . they'll get theirs!" Then they calmly get on with their day. Be careful, though, because as you will soon find out, these seemingly harmless groups often house the company's Level 9's (Paranoia), and these guys and gals are not only very demotivating, but are at the risk of going Level 10 (Insanity) at any time (read on!).

Level 3 symptoms include:

- High frustration levels
- Territory dominance
- Frequent use of "if only . . . " statements
- Random threats to partake of Level 4 activities

. . . when Sheldon met Christine

Sheldon and Christine both came to RTI from successful careers with other manufacturing companies. They have 12 and 9 years of experience respectively, and know all the ins and outs of corporate survival. They each hit the ground running in middle management at RTI, but soon found out that the depth and competence of their staffs and superiors were not all they were cracked up to be. Sheldon's Quality Control department is critical to the profitability of every production line in the plant, but he is forever fighting to get approval on new testing equipment available to more accurately measure tight tolerance milling operations. Sure, the existing devices work, but he has presented several formal proposals showing cost savings of 15 to 20 percent per year in improved setup times and reduced scrap. It always comes down to budget concerns controlled by supervisors too far removed, it seems, to appreciate the importance of his concerns. At least that's what their lack of response tells him.

Christine's call center takes upwards of 1,000 information requests and phone orders per day. She has successfully cut costs and improved response time without additional staff for the past two years, but now is struggling to add three more, well-justified, technical support people. Although Christine's thoroughly researched and professionally written proposal was immediately approved by her boss, it is bogged down in a newly formed budget committee that is considering outsourcing both her call center and the company's mailroom to a very competitively priced vendor. She is familiar with that particular vendor from her previous job, but is finding it difficult to convince management that, while they may be able to handle the mail room function, RTI would be better off keeping internal control over the phones. Her rationale regarding both service and security is well founded, but again her proposal falls to the distant and unresponsive budget committee for approval.

Sheldon and Christine have begun to share each others' frustrations, griping and complaining in impromptu discussions during breaks. They can sometimes even be coaxed into various "grumble gatherings" and "threaten throngs" to vent some of their disapproval for the way that management is holding up progress for the company. Both of these employees are on the fast track with RTI, but often find their enthusiasm curtailed by policies and slow, bureaucratic committees that they see as doing nothing more than making an already tough job even harder.

They are classic Levels 3's, at constant risk of losing ground to the escape of Level 4 (Escape), the discomfort of Level 5 (Gut Check), the temporary relief of Level 6 (Class Clown), or even the panacea of Level 7 (Apathy) over time.

Perhaps they will be able to convince an overly vertical management structure to allow increased lower level decision-making in certain areas. They might be able to infiltrate some of the newly formed committees, so their ideas can be more readily heard. Hopefully, they will become part of the solution, rather than part of the problem, by keeping their cool and working with management to improve the work environment within their circle of influence.

Employee Perspective

While it is probably becoming obvious to you already that none of the *Ten Levels* represent healthy places to spend your career, Level 3 (Griping and Complaining) is by far the most promising place to find yourself. It means you still have a burning desire to achieve success. You are a dedicated employee with determination, pride and the grit to keep plugging. The periodic ventilation therapy you partake of is a way of letting off a little steam, so you can get back to work. The danger lies in the tendency for these bouts of shared frustration to become a habit, robbing you of productive time and draining your energy.

Because a department's Level 3's are often also its leaders, you are probably one of the people most likely to spearhead the introduction of *The Vocational Shrink* to your fellow employees. The good news is, the time and interest you put into sharing the *Ten Levels*, and helping others to become aware of their habits, will reduce some of the time spent griping and complaining. That's the secret to survival in Level 3; you must constantly be on the lookout for intriguing, new challenges to get you pumped up again. The beauty of *The Vocational Shrink* is that this exercise can have a lasting impact on you, your associates, and your managers. If you participate in helping others – as well as yourself – identify and escape your levels, the results will be a permanently improved workplace with more productivity, opportunity, and fun – just what Level 3's (or better said, ex-Level 3's) will thrive on!

Management Perspective

Your department's Level 3's are usually the most active, demanding and creative folks, so they will naturally be the first people you will look to for reactions to *The Vocational Shrink – The Game*. The longer they have been hanging out in Level 3 (Griping and Complaining), the more likely it is that they will initially be pessimistic about the Game. However, it is their need to be productive and moving ahead with their career – ambition is their soft spot. If you can hook them with the benefits, get them to participate in developing departmental goals. If you win them over to the long-term benefits for themselves, as well as the company, they'll help you rally the rest of the troops. Get these folks on your team and they'll row the boat for you, allowing you to spend valuable time in your macro mode, viewing the department as a whole during the transition.

Because this book's companion game and training can be used as a non-threatening way for opening people up to the wasteful ways of their favorite levels, it can give you the opportunity to periodically break up a "gripe group" and finesse the Level 3's back into action. Remember, all of the levels are habits, so even the most well-meaning employees will backslide from time to time. The beauty of the Game is that everyone buys into the objectives, so they can't fight too hard when their Level 3 behavior is later pointed out.

I suggest you take it easy on Level 3's with regards to pointing out their griping and complaining behaviors as the Game progresses. These kinds of people pride themselves on self discipline and you'll find they won't need to be reminded often to think positively and remember the big picture. These are the future leaders of this company, along with you, so remind yourself that you are better off working with them than against them. Many a frustrated Level 3 who leaves their current company, comes back as a competitor; if so, they'll be out to get you with a vengeance and they're armed with a whole lot of knowledge about your weaknesses! Best to win these people over and work with them to make all of their roles more rewarding right there at RTI.

The Ten Levels

DISBELIEF	1	6	CLASS CLOWN
NODDING & AGREEING	2	7	APATHY
GRIPING & COMPLAINING		8	SURRENDER
ESCAPE	4	9	PARANOIA
~~GUT CHECK~~		10	INSANITY

Chapter 4
Level 4 – Escape

Here's a tricky level. Many of your friends, even people in your favorite "beef bevy," are disguised Level 3's (Griping and Complaining), slowly slipping into Level 4, and they probably aren't even aware of it. The pressures of Level 3 are simply too tough for the average person to cope with for extended periods of time. They "escape," sadly, into Level 4. Drinking (or other mind-numbing options) starts out as a social activity, but can change into a habit, often in proportion to the amount of frustration one has felt combined with a person's "tolerance" or threshold for dependency.

Those harmless trips to the local pub for a beer are the breeding ground of Level 4 mentality. Be particularly wary if those trips begin to occur before work or during lunch. In many cases, particularly in a social setting, Level 4's seem a lot like Level 9's (Paranoia). The difference is, a Level 4 still has a realistic chance to pull out of it, while a true Level 9 is only going to be helped by extensive therapy, and unfortunately, their acceptance of professional help is rare.

Level 4 symptoms include:

- Reminiscing about childhood experiences
- A short (or shorter) fuse

- Making mistakes out of haste or carelessness
- Getting a Mohawk

Not all Level 3's (Griping and Complaining) move on to Level 4 for relief; how nice to know, you may be saying. The rest of us can look forward to crawling through Levels 5 (Gut Check) and 6 (Class Clown) to the poten-

. . . you know Chris in Shipping

tial tranquility of Level 7 (Apathy).

Chris has been in the shipping and receiving area as long as anyone can remember. As one of Mr. Randaletti's first group of employees hired as the business began to grow, Chris really knows the inner workings of RTI.

As an early department head, much of the credit for breaking shipping records was given to Chris. This was an employee with an unlimited future, maybe not as a designer or engineer, but as a top performer in the production and distribution end of the business. Chris was always willing to lend a hand, and took part in many of the company's extra curricular activities. Captain of the darts team, top bowler with a 200+ average, scrappy pitcher for the softball team, and the best setter the RTI volleyball team ever had.

All of these events ended with harmless trips to the local bars in the area. As the years went by, Chris began to slide into a regime involving more frequent and longer lasting bar (escape) visits. After work is a given. During lunch . . . well, more often than anybody knows. That goal of quitting smoking never quite happened. After 15 years, this lifestyle is beginning to take its toll. Don't get me wrong, Chris is still a hard working and dedicated employee, but that "Johnny on the spot" attitude has diminished. That early morning reliability has dragged into an 8:45 to 4:30 schedule. Age has crept up and begun to show the accumulated signs of the physical abuse and inconsistent sleep patterns.

Because of his time with the company and unquestioned skill, it is tough for management to confront this slow decline by Chris, however it is becoming a point of discussion during annual reviews. A Level 4 can be turned around but, as with any addictive habit pattern, it must begin with the victim's acknowledgement of the disease and a true desire to change. Hopefully, for RTI and Chris, this will happen before declining health makes it too late to turn back.

Employee Perspective

Let's be honest; nobody plans to slip into chemical dependency. Obviously, many people have not been as successful as they'd like in their attempts to avoid this stress-induced dilemma. Like any addiction, the first and most important step is to admit it, so here's your chance. *The Vocational Shrink – The Game* was designed to allow employees a safe haven to honestly evaluate their workplace habits and their consequences. If your employer has provided you this opportunity, you probably have one of the best possible scenarios to courageously and candidly address your status and make the changes needed to get your life and work back on track.

Because of the number of different chemicals that make up Level 4 (Escape) behavior, and the fact that everyone handles these things in different ways, our goal is not to pigeonhole symptoms or suggest a blanket diagnosis. This is a personal issue and will be dealt with only when you are ready. All I can say with certainty is that you have a better chance of succeeding in your attempt to battle this disease (or habit that could lead to a disease) and keep your job, if you confront it in the context of *The Vocational Shrink*.

Most Level 4's are actually Level 3's (Griping and Complaining) that got side tracked during one of their runs around the 3-6 Loop (see Chapter 11 – Cyclic Trends). This means that you were probably a valuable, highly functional asset to your firm before your slide and that you can easily become that kind of employee again. Most people root for the underdog and besting chemical dependency, as common as it is in our society; it's one of the places that carries forgiveness and congratulations to those who are fortunate enough to recover.

Management Perspective

As important as it is for human beings to help one another, your role in rescuing your Level 4 employees carries with it a multiple benefit. Sure, it would give you a feeling of pride and accomplishment to participate in helping anyone beat an addiction but, as we mentioned above, many Level 4's began as valuable, productive employees. *The Vocational Shrink – The Game* may turn out to be effective for you in reaching Level 4, or borderline Level 4 employees, than those in any other level. Level 1's (Disbelief) aren't experienced enough to really "get it" yet, so are easy to get motivated, but are also the easiest folks to replace. Level 2's (Nodding and Agreeing), at least the long-term ones, have a history of defensive behavior and will tend to always be hard to win over to team play. Level 3's (Griping and Complaining) often believe they are bigger than all of this, bullet-proof, so to speak. Level 5 (Gut Check) and up is where physiological issues come into play, so many of these people have more baggage to carry on their trip back to cooperative work life.

Early stage Level 4's are a worthy and realistic group for you to help as a manager. You get to enjoy the dual blessing of saving a friend from a declining downward spiral and, if you are successful, you also get an experienced, quality employee who will make an immediate positive contribution to your department. It is likely that they will actually come back even stronger, having skirted the edge of disaster. These people have the potential to lead others, both by example and through their fresh enthusiasm. You are wielding some great power here, because these Level 4's are usually pretty popular folks and carry a lot of others in their wake.

The danger, of course, is that some Level 4's (Escape) are simply not salvageable, so you are taking a chance. I don't know if there is a way to estimate the possibility of bringing a borderline Level 4 back, however, I strongly believe that using *The Vocational Shrink – The Game* as a way of getting their attention and offering them a safe vehicle maximizes your odds of success. While no substitute for professional help, it's definitely worth a try, as the alternative is obvious and inevitable.

Chapter 5
Level 5 – Gut Check

Level 5, the mystery level. Generally, you aren't aware that your buddy is a Level 5 unless he or she tells you. Level 5 introduces annoyances like: lower back aches, indigestion, ulcers, high blood pressure, rapid heart rate, and other intestinal aches and pains not easily distinguishable by your Level 3 peers (who may be Level 5's too, for all you know).

Level 5 symptoms include:

- That glassy-eyed look of uncertainty as in, "I've already gone four times this morning, but I just might need another trip . . ."
- Lack of motivation
- Reduced interest in tackling new challenges
- Holding stomach (or side) and wincing

Obviously, an individual's pain threshold dictates how long they can remain in Level 5 while keeping everyone else convinced they're still as much a Level 3 as ever. The damage is done either way and soon the mind succumbs to the discomfort. On to Level 6 (Class Clown), you lucky thing you!

. . . superwoman Gwen

Gwen literally holds the Return Goods Department together. She has been promoted four times in the last ten years, and has shown no signs of shrinking from any new challenge. While occasionally succumbing to the allure of Level 3 (Griping and Complaining) "put-down posses", Gwen has been a model employee in this fast-paced, high-growth corporation.

Recently, Gwen has been having some stomach symptoms that have caught her by surprise. The workload and stress don't seem to have increased, but her energy level just isn't what it used to be. Maybe it's the coffee, or the infrequent, less-than-nutritious meals grabbed on the run, but she is going through more TUMS® than normal and is experiencing more frequent bouts of intestinal rebellion.

No one seems to notice the difference. Gwen is so good at what she does, and has such a strong work ethic, that she handles the inconvenience of these new gut check challenges without missing a beat. Because her performance and attitude remain strong, she is able to continue on without attracting any management attention. This is the beginning of Level 5 (Gut Check) for Gwen, and it will only get worse if not attended to soon.

The normal pattern, if she doesn't change her work habits, will be increased internal discomfort, additional medications, less energy and, ultimately, a decline in performance. Along the way, she will constantly be at risk of sliding into the mental vacation of Level 6 (Class Clown) and beginning a series of 3-6 Loops (see Chapter 11, Cyclic Trends). As a 3-6 Looper, she then inherits the potential of taking a permanent escape to Level 4, or giving up to the tranquility of Level 7 (Apathy).

Hard working Level 5's like Gwen need to be handled just like Level 3's, because they are often indistinguishable from them. They maintain the same dedicated, aggressive and professional tendencies that have made them successful, but are at greater risk of falling prey to other dangers within the system, once the Level 5 symptoms begin to eat away at their concentration and resilience.

Management's ability to identify and work with the Level 3's and Level 5's in their organization will have immediate impact on productivity and morale throughout the entire staff. These people represent the leaders and motivators of your company, and the others will tend to respond to their guidance. By nature, they are also the most responsive to new opportunities and changes that simplify the systems that so often restrict their growth.

Employee Perspective

The ball is really in your court here, as a new Level 5. You have probably had conflicting thoughts about the increased frequency and intensity of your intestinal symptoms, but may well have been able to hide them from your other Level 3 coworkers (Griping and Complaining). I can guarantee you this, however; you can't win this one by ignoring it and covering it up.

Early Level 5 (Gut Check) annoyances are your wake-up call that the stress of Level 3 is beginning to take its toll. If you are new to Level 5, then this material has gotten into your hands at just the right time, because you can simply follow the previous Level 3 advice and nobody will be the wiser. Not that there is any embarrassment to the confrontation of physical limitations but, depending on your age, you may just not want to be seen in that group yet.

If you are farther along in your Level 5 journey and are already well schooled in the use of various over-the-counter remedies, then you'll have to consider more serious life-changing decisions. I would venture to guess that your diet and exercise routine is not as it should be, your weight and blood pressure may not be optimal, and you may just not give a darn! Go ahead . . . vent, justify, make whatever excuses you need to, and when you're done, *The Vocational Shrink* will be waiting!

Okay, ready to listen now? Here's the deal; no matter what kind of shape you are in or have ever been in, it is an undisputed fact that getting a handle on your food and beverage intake and getting your body in some semblance of shape will do wonders in combating the stress demons that are eating your insides. I'm not going to go into a full health and fitness program discussion here, but will make three points and one suggestion:

1. Cardiovascular exercise (anything that takes your heart rate up to a minimum of 60% of your Maximum Heart Rate for 20 to 30 minutes at a time, three to four days a week, is a great way to get your circulatory system in shape.

2. Weightlifting that works individual muscle groups to a point of exhaustion will break down muscle tissue and allow it to rebuild larger and stronger. Muscle is where the enzymes that control metabolism live, so the more "lean muscle mass" you have, the more efficiently your body burns calories all the time.

3. What you eat and drink, and when you do it is the secret to the whole thing. The word "DIET" is a bad word (anything with the word "DIE" in it,

can't be too uplifting!), but what it actually refers to is "What You Eat". Add to that "When You Eat" and "What you Drink" and you are there.

I have a wonderful story about my own fitness journey that I'm saving for my next book, but I will suggest this resource. *Body for Life*[2] by Bill Phillips is the best book I have read that really makes sense, seems doable, and doesn't turn you into a gym rat. As a matter of fact, the more complex and time consuming your health and fitness routine becomes, the more likely you won't stick to it . . . just like all the diets you've ever tried!

Getting a grip on your health is always a good idea, but Level 5 (Gut Check) seems to be a particularly good time for many of us to finally take it seriously. You may be experiencing physical complications for the first time in a basically healthy life. You may also still be young enough to be willing to take a run at it. Level 8's (Decline & Surrender) are often older and have truly debilitating complications on top of the simple Level 5 stuff, so they find it harder to look realistically at fitness programs. This is the stage in your life and career where you are being given the prodding you need, before irreversible problems have taken away the window of opportunity.

Level 5 is a bit of a resting place in the *Ten Levels*, perhaps an unintentional one, but a change of pace, no less. It represents the perfect time in your career to honestly look at your health, your diet and exercise habits, and to consider some long-term changes. This may well be looked back on as a significant turning point in your life.

---

2 *Body for Life*, Bill Phillips, HarperCollins Publishers 1999

Management Perspective

Next to salvaging borderline Level 4's (Escape), your best use of *The Vocational Shrink* will be in reestablishing positive, productive and healthy goals with your Level 5's. Level 3 (Griping and Complaining) and Level 5 (Gut Check) make up the bulk of your department's employees – perhaps as much as 75-80%. Because it is often impossible to differentiate Level 5's from Level 3's, you do best to simply consider them all Level 3's until you are made aware of, or notice, the symptoms of a Level 5 ailment.

The good news it that you can keep it simple and deal with them pretty much the same way. Start out using the Management Perspective for Level 3, then identify the Level 5's as they show themselves. Actually, the health and fitness suggestions for Level 5 will not be wasted on Level 3's, as they will be there sooner or later if they stay on the Level 3 (Griping and Complaining) track. These two levels house your greatest asset and until the Level 5 symptoms arrived, they were cut from identical cloth. As a supervisor, you are very likely a Level 3 or perhaps Level 5 yourself . . . or have been, or will be. This is where the aggressive, positive, motivated, take-charge people cut their teeth, so you must have had some of these characteristics to have been promoted to management.

You may find that advocating a healthy diet and exercise lifestyle, then participating along with your employees, will benefit you as much as them, while offering a way of building camaraderie and mutual respect. The two most important ingredients in good human relations are respect and genuine caring. Recommending something to your subordinates, then participating in it with them, is a great way to enhance both of these goals in your workplace. Having lost 25 pounds while making health and fitness a part of my normal routine has been immensely helpful for me, and good health allows me to be a more credible consultant, parent, husband, father and worker.

Level 5 (Gut Check) is the turning point in the *Ten Levels*. Level 6 (Class Clown) offers one last bastion of hope, but beyond that it becomes a slippery slope. You can burn a tremendous amount of energy and resources trying to revitalize these folks. These active, creative, proud and experienced people are your foundation to the turnaround you strive for in using tools like *The Vocational Shrink*. Getting employees on board by Level 5 is one of the keys to maximizing the effectiveness of this program.

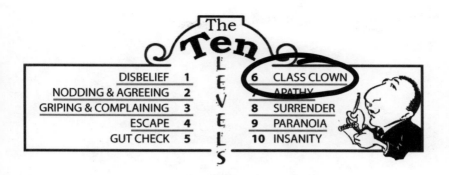

DISBELIEF	1		6	CLASS CLOWN
NODDING & AGREEING	2		~~APATHY~~	
GRIPING & COMPLAINING	3		8	SURRENDER
ESCAPE	4		9	PARANOIA
GUT CHECK	5		10	INSANITY

Chapter 6
Level 6 – Class Clown

For some reason, the mind is subtly altered by the first five Levels of Workplace Disillusionment. Maybe it's the frustration of Levels 1, 2, and 3; the involvement, or fear of involvement, in Level 4; or the discomfort and secrecy of Level 5. It's hard to say for sure. Regardless, Level 6 becomes the "catch-all" for the slightly demented peculiarities that haunt the mind of the war-weary employee after years of struggling for fulfillment in our country's factories and offices.

Level 6 symptoms include:

- A false sense of security
- A nonchalant, almost jovial attitude
- Doing imitations of fellow workers
- Mistelling old jokes and humming obscure tunes

Although Level 6's help to liven up the place, you must be cognizant of the fact that they are sensitive and should not be antagonized. Your best response is to treat them like any of your Level 3 (Griping and Complaining) buddies, unless they directly interfere with your job function. Direct confrontation could result in their transference to Level 7 (Apathy), or . . . gasp, beyond!

lightin half tone

... Quick-Wit Gene ...

Gene has always had a quick wit and good sense of humor. His talent and educational credentials, with a Masters Degree in Metallurgy and 10 years of experience, have never been questioned, but lately he seems more interested in the joke he heard the other day, or the next gag he plans to pull, than in the status of the shop's Heat Treat facilities.

Don't get me wrong – he's not out sabotaging the annealing furnaces or tripping people while they are carrying racks of hot forgings, but his attitude seems more intent on being a class clown than work. Gene is a blast to be around and is very popular at all company functions. He can do an imitation of Fred, the vacuum furnace department lead man, better than Fred can do himself!

Gene has not changed his work ethic or ability to juggle the never-ending changes and rush jobs that continually pour into his department. He just seems to have lost his intensity and the furrowed brow that was always one of his distinguishing characteristics. While no one can show evidence that this new, upbeat, almost loosy-goosy style has affected his performance, it is making some people nervous. It's almost like a different Gene, and while he is more fun to be around, there is the tendency for everyone to find themselves waiting for the other shoe to drop.

Unlike Level 5 (Gut Check), which is often undistinguishable for long periods of time, Level 6 (Class Clown) is easy to spot. It is usually a rather big departure from the victim's normal work style, and is often loud and attention-getting. Because it is associated with fun, and is usually a stress reducer for everyone involved, Level 6 is not seen as a negative habit pattern at all. What's wrong with having a little fun at work, anyway?

The problem is that Level 6er's have not become that way as a healthy alternative to acting too serious on the job. They have succumbed to Class Clown status as a defense against the stresses and frustrations of Level 3 (Griping and Complaining) and the inevitable discomforts of Level 5 (Gut Check). What could be seen as a positive change of attitudes is really a resting place where the bedraggled high achiever regains his or her strength until a sufficiently intriguing new project responsibility drags them back down to Level 3. Then, unless something has changed in company politics, the cycle begins again.

If Level 6 becomes too much fun, and a "Level 3 instigating challenge" does not present itself soon enough, our happy-go-lucky employee begins to risk falling prey to Level 7 (Apathy). As retirement approaches, experience in Level 6 (Class Clown) can actually expedite the transition to Level 7 (Apathy). The reduced stress and free use of the imagination can make daydreams of the cabin on the lake and sipping iced tea sound more inviting than that next big project. Here is where sentient management must step in and deftly lead this droll, but misfocused, player back into the game.

This is a very critical turning point in the *Ten Levels of Workplace Disillusionment*. As you will see, once an employee enters Level 7 (Apathy), there is usually no turning back. A Level 6 can easily be coaxed back into the fray, but a true Level 7 has only retirement or Level 8 (Decline & Surrender) to look forward to.

Employee Perspective

Congratulations, you've selected one of the more fun places to rest up on the *Ten Levels of Workplace Disillusionment*. Unlike Level 5 (Gut Check), where the need for a vacation is forced upon you by bodily discomfort, Level 6 (Class Clown) is a departure from the seriousness and stress of everyday work chosen in a somewhat brazen, "what-the-heck" manner. Although Level 6 is a choice, it is really a choice made between several evils.

You probably got here because of the stress that built up in Level 3 (Griping and Complaining), an aversion to the chemical alternatives of Level 4 (Escape) or as a way to skip experiencing Level 5 (Gut Check) symptoms. Or, perhaps it was your method for dealing with Level 5 symptoms. Either way, you're not dealing with stress in a totally healthy way, even though it tends to be more personally and socially acceptable to become the Level 6 (Class Clown) than to self destruct or stay angry. Does that sound like you?

Going to Level 6 (Class Clown) from Level 3 (Griping and Complaining) and back is so common that we have a name for it – the "3-6 Loop" (see Chapter 11 – Cyclic Trends). In other words, you're not alone! There are some striking positives and negatives to dwelling in Level 6 for too long, so I'll describe a way to keep the good and drop the bad as you get a grip on why Level 6 (Class Clown) is your drug of choice.

Let's face it, there's nothing wrong with a good sense of humor. The jokers and clowns make work fun and keep folks smiling; that's the good part, so don't lose that. The fact that many go there as an escape to avoid dealing with their stresses and frustrations is the negative side of this characteristic. Too much joking and playing can cause you to slip in your job performance and get to a point where you don't even care. The key here is to sort the wheat from the chaff. Use your new habit of fun-loving adventure to relax, but also remind yourself that this is just laughter therapy to help unwind and refocus on your job. Because most Level 6er's are not there long term, but simply as a reprieve from job stress, it is probably the least dangerous level. However, like the other exit levels – Level 2 (Nodding and Agreeing), Level 4 (Escape), Level 7 (Apathy) and Level 9 (Paranoia) – it's easy to think you're in control and that you can quit any time you want, when you are actually getting sucked into the comfort of habit.

Have fun in Level 6 when needed, but make sure to test yourself regularly by buckling down to your work aggressively and keeping the sense of humor at the same time. This is as close as you can get to a glimpse of life outside of the *Ten Levels* before actually breaking free!

Management Perspective

The problem with your Level 6 (Class Clown) employees is that they are just a hoot to hang out with. It is tough to be the spoiler, so management usually looks the other way, justifies them as good for the department's morale, and lives with it, as long as they don't fall into sexual harassment or some other unacceptable level of fun.

When you can identify a Level 5 (Gut Check) they are a sitting duck . . . because their intestinal discomfort slows them down and makes them ripe for talk of change. Level 6's, on the other hand, are much more elusive. They aren't really doing anything wrong and most of them are still productive. So what do you do to address this behavior? First, remind yourself that you're probably dealing with a 3-6 Looper (Chapter 11 – Cyclic Trends), so they will be a Level 3 (Griping and Complaining) again soon. Second, be cognizant of the fact that they are now at the final "recoverable" level, so if you don't get them now before they get too close to retirement age, you risk losing them to Level 7 (Apathy). In Level 7, you'll have no choice but to just make the person comfortable and keep them from infecting the rest of the troops.

I suggest you treat Level 6's just like Level 3's and simply wait for them to come around the Loop to Level 3 again. If you confront the behavior change or try to point out sags in their performance, they'll deny it and it will quickly degenerate into a "he said, she said" mode. Most Level 6's (Class Clown) are just tired Level 3's anyway, so getting them to be part of the solution rather than dwelling on how they may be part of the problem has a much better chance of success. Success breeds success, so as you get other employees on board, your Level 6's will not only be drawn to the enthusiasm, but will make the whole game a lot more fun.

The older your Level 6, the more careful you have to be, however, because the lure of Level 7 (Apathy) and The Fulcrum (Chapter 12 – Self-Maintaining Trends) begins to compete for their attention. I suggest you keep them laughing while you subtly invite them to participate and even help lead the new vision of the department. Like Level 4 (Escape) folks, Level 6's tend to be pretty popular around the office and can bring a number of others over with them when you get them involved.

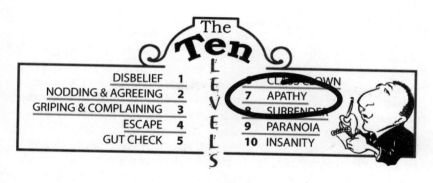

DISBELIEF	1			CLASS CLOWN
NODDING & AGREEING	2		7	APATHY
GRIPING & COMPLAINING	3		8	SURRENDER
ESCAPE	4		9	PARANOIA
GUT CHECK	5		10	INSANITY

Chapter 7
Level 7 – Apathy

Just when you were starting to consider moving to a small town in Wyoming and becoming a convenience store clerk, there's a lull in the storm. Level 7 houses the fortunate few who honestly don't care. They smile and leisurely go about their business. They tend to move in predictable patterns from day to day. Their reactions are slow, deliberate and very professional, if necessary, but without ambition and drive. Let's be reasonable – if they get too fired up, they'll risk falling back to Level 3 (Griping and Complaining)!

The problem with Level 7 is that it's incredibly hard to stay there. You sit on the fulcrum, not wanting to slide back to the 3-6 Loop (see Chapter 11, Cyclic Trends) or fall over toward a slow slide into the oblivion of Levels 8, 9 or 10.

Level 7 symptoms include:

- A relaxed, almost lazy demeanor, with an occasional noncommittal chuckle
- Avoidance of confrontation with the innate ability to look through the situation to blue skies on the horizon
- Narcolepsy
- Knowing (to the hour) how long they have until retirement

Level 7's cannot remain Level 7's for long periods of time. Most were once strong Level 3's and can be drawn back down periodically if tricked into assuming responsibility by shrewd management. I have only known one who made it to retirement as a true Level 7, and the problem with that is it's hard to conjure up much ambition during retirement, after so much practice at being genuinely apathetic. But that's another book . . .

. . . Heerrre'sss Harry!

Harry is known throughout the industry as one of the most innovative product designers around. He's responsible for many of RTI's early successes, and a number of his components are still being produced for major customers. Harry has always been one of the first people in the office, and is a real team player.

Over the past couple of years, however, as new computer-aided design equipment has begun to replace the drawing boards in the department, and new blood has come in along with the new VP, Harry seems to be slowing down a little. He has always been an avid fisherman, but now his stories about the week at Lake Powell or the deep sea experience in Cabo are told with more frequency and emotion. With retirement only three years (two years, ten months, 13 days, and 2½ hours, to be exact) away, Harry's mind wanders.

He can often be seen during lunch time or breaks, thumbing through an *American Angler* magazine or looking at the current month on his Fishing Facts calendar with a glazed look and a sigh. His work is still top notch and he is about as efficient as anyone in the department, but the thrill is gone. Harry was a classic Level 3 (Griping and Complaining) during his early career, one of the best, or so it seemed, at handling the pressure of corporate politics. No one really knows how much of the last few years were spent in Level 3, and how much in Level 5 (Gut Check), but Harry has finally reached the pinnacle of his trip through the system. He was never very comfortable as a Level 6 (Class Clown), although we all remember times when he did go there for some comfort.

The combination of time, stress and pending retirement have finally taken him to a new place, a balancing act called Level 7 (Apathy). It's not that he doesn't care – Harry is a true company man who would never do anything to hurt RTI or its employees. He has just lost the grit to keep fighting new battles, and the reality of his retirement dreams are becoming more and more alluring to him now.

Similar to Ray, our Level 2 (Nodding and Agreeing) example, Harry has earned his place in upper management and is not at risk of being replaced, as long as Bob still thinks he's cutting it. The difference is that he does not fear his fate, he only has to ride out a little more time doing what he knows how to do and living off his past glory. This is a far less frightening position to be in than Level 2, however, and over time it can lead to a pretty lackadaisical attitude. No more real challenges, no more big successes or big failures either. Harry has to be careful to avoid getting too wrapped up in new projects, because he can't let himself get pulled back down into Level 3 (Griping and Complaining). It's not the excitement of a new challenge as much as it is the inevitable ride back through the discomfort of Level 5 that he just can't seem to work up enough energy to confront again.

Better to just bide his time, count the days, keep it all in perspective and dream. All we can hope for is that Harry makes it to that blessed day, and has enough health and motivation left to really enjoy the realization of those dreams and his well-earned retirement. The objective is virtuous, but the odds are, unfortunately, against him as he burns up valuable vitality riding The Fulcrum (see Chapter 11 – Cyclic Trends), and avoiding the fire of Level 8 (Decline & Surrender).

Employee Perspective

You never planned to be here in Level 7, I'll bet. Interestingly enough, in the time you spend reading this sentence, you may not be there any more! Level 7 is the peak of *Ten Levels of Workplace Disillusionment*, not Level 10 (Insanity) like you might think. Before Level 7 lie all of the grit and growth levels filled with employees striving to find their place in the workforce. Beyond Level 7 are the declining valleys from which few return. Balancing Level 7 is extremely difficult; virtually impossible for an extended period of time.

You are trying to avoid all of the frustration and stress of the first six levels (where you have spent the majority of your career) and ride out the remainder of your career, but are petrified of falling victim to Level 8 (Decline & Surrender), Level 9 (Paranoia), or Level 10 (Insanity). Good luck, you are now rolling the dice. Here are a few questions to ask yourself, if you want to take this gamble:

1. How long is it until you can retire?
2. Do you think you can actually last that long in Level 7?
3. If you can't, which way will you fall?
4. Then what???

Here's the Catch 22. If you had the strength to continue the battle, you would still be running the 3-6 Loop (Chapter 11 – Cyclic Trends). If you really don't have the strength, you are at high risk of falling over into Level 8 or beyond. This is a dangerous quandary and nobody can, or wants, to help you. Not that they don't like you or care, but the truth is, everyone is secretly envious of Level 7. We all wish we could hang out there, but know it is a mine field. While one part of us hopes you can pull it off, another part of us hopes you fail so that we can feel better about our lack of courage.

If we really had any guts, we would be honest with you and suggest you go back and read the list again. Then, we'd suggest that you measure your Level 7 plan carefully and make sure you can time this final dash to freedom properly. My personal suggestion is to do everything you can to make it as short as possible, because if you fail, it will be at least emotionally draining and at most terminal!

Management Perspective

This is a tough one, however relax; you will experience few true Level 7's (Apathy) in your career. Even the ones that claim to be Level 7 are probably just Level 3's (Griping and Complaining) with a pipe dream, or Level 4's (Escape) who had one extra martini at lunch, maybe Level 5's (Gut Check) trying to ease the pain, or Level 6's (Class Clown) trying to fool themselves. An actual Level 7 will need to be tested over time. If and when you find a true Level 7, you owe it to them, yourself, and the rest of the department to do whatever it takes to help them make it safely (and quickly) to retirement. They have paid their dues, deserve to break free without losing face, and stand to be of no value to you in enhancing your other employee's morale or team spirit.

In the meantime, treat them like your Level 3's and 5's and see what happens. If they are going to fall out of Level 7, better for it to be back into the grind than into the abyss. You have nothing to lose and no other options until you are genuinely convinced they are an actual Level 7. Then, go to upper management and make sure they are assisted to as rapid a retirement as possible. They will benefit from having more time left to enjoy the rest of their life of leisure, you will be able to get back to more important management responsibilities, you'll be cutting costs, and your employees will avoid the needless distraction.

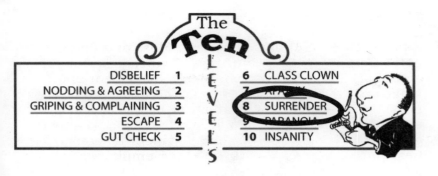

DISBELIEF	1	6	CLASS CLOWN
NODDING & AGREEING	2	7	APATHY
GRIPING & COMPLAINING	3	8	SURRENDER
ESCAPE	4	9	PARANOIA
GUT CHECK	5	10	INSANITY

Chapter 8
Level 8 – Decline and Surrender

Your Level 8 is usually a person who bounced in and out of Level 7 (Apathy) for a while and just couldn't handle the boredom. Like Level 5 (Griping and Complaining), Level 8 involves the body responding to past frustrations and mistreatment. Level 8's often appear tired and unhealthy, and have many pills, ointments, inhalants, and lotions in their desks. Don't get a Level 8 confused with someone who actually has an allergy or skin rash, as you could blow a perfectly good diagnosis.

Level 8 symptoms include:

- Hair loss (not normal baldness, but random patches)
- Twitching, scratching, and a sickly look
- A recurring, pathetic sigh
- Fatigue

Level 8's may appear confused, because they have made the decision to move on with their careers (rather than struggle to stay in Level 7 when they are truly not apathetic enough to pull it off), but can't muster the energy to take another run at Level 3 (Griping and Complaining). Watch them closely – some could be handy to know. They usually have a lot of valuable experience and little to lose. If they are lucky, they will retire before having to deal with Levels 9 (Paranoia) or 10 (Insanity).

... meet the "nice-guy", Sid

Sid is the kind of guy who you would confidently go to if you had $5,000 bucks you needed to have guarded for a week. He is calm, friendly, low key, and impeccably honest. Not any ball of fire, but reliable, fair, and with a wealth of knowledge about all aspects of the Inspection and Testing Department.

Fifteen years with NASA, then twelve more at RTI; this guy has been around a lot of pretty cool manufacturing processes and fascinating development projects in his day. A lot like our Level 7 (Apathy) friend Harry, Sid rode the fast lane for a long time prior to slowly settling into his anticipated smooth ride to retirement.

Unfortunately, Sid was unable to properly time his final kick into Level 7 with his ability to handle true apathy. In the same way the go-getter Level 3 unwittingly slips into Level 5 while nobody notices, our seemingly composed ninth-inning closer falls prey to Level 8. Unlike the internal complications of Level 5 (Gut Check), the Level 8 (Decline and Surrender) victim experiences more visible signs of the battle. Rashes, hair loss, and an overall sickly look often begin to take over as daily concerns. Today's medical community offers a plethora of remedies and comforts that can manage the symptoms for quite a long time, but the inevitable damage is done. That blessed retirement is being shortened, eaten away by the very institution that made it possible.

If Sid is lucky, his career will be completed before the physical limitations restrict too many of his retirement plans. Often, this is not the case. As much as everyone hopes to leave at the top of their game, it is not as easy as it seems. Higher pay, bigger responsibilities, and the realization of job opportunities only imagined earlier in their career make it hard for successful achievers to leave the system while they are still on their game. By the time the real end is near, they are left to balance the time that remains with a gnawing realization that they have passed their prime, and everyone knows it.

That may or may not be true, but if they believe it to be, their trip through Level 7 carries with it greater risk of the body reacting with Level 8 symptoms and a rapid slide begins. It is ironic, but the more accomplished an employee becomes during his or her career, the more difficult it is to pull off a judicious exit from the game. The same character strengths that are responsible for the past success and duration of a celebrated career make the timely and effectual acceptance of Level 7 (Apathy) more prone to failure. It is simply too hard to make a transition to true apathy while still in the environment that carries all the memories of enthusiastic accomplishment. The problem lies in the inability to anticipate the length of time that this balancing act can be performed, and use of that knowledge to choose the best time to change gears.

This is one of the built-in dilemmas often associated with a corporate career. It can bring some of the greatest joy and pride in life, but there is not a clear-cut exit strategy available to many participants, and logic is often weaker than emotion when considering retirement options. When left too long, the system that creates an employee's success often ends up being responsible for their unflattering and early demise.

Employee Perspective

Level 8 is not a fun level, so I'll be frank with you and not joke around. You don't want to stay here long. Anyone who reaches Level 8 is not a spring chicken and is here for one of two reasons. Either you hit Level 7 (Apathy) too soon to ride it out all the way to retirement, or you burned out and just have more time left on the job than you do energy. Either way, you are not doing yourself or the company any good by hanging around a moment longer than necessary. Realize that this is not a critique of your talent, experience, integrity or company loyalty. You simply have gone beyond your prime and need to move on while you still can.

The first thing to do is get a medical check-up and see what is actually ailing you. If it is stress related and not permanent or terminal, do whatever you can to retire, get into a healthy lifestyle and start enjoying the rest of your life. If it is irreversible, you still owe it to yourself and your family to get the most you can out of the rest of your life. Spend time with your spouse, children, grandchildren and friends. You've worked long enough and you don't owe anything to anybody. Face it, work's killing you and if you don't do something soon, it will finish the job.

Can Level 8 (Decline & Surrender) happen to a younger person or one further down the chain of command? Not likely, as Level 8 symptoms only come as a last result of many failed attempts at seeking a more pleasant level or escaping the *Ten Levels* altogether. Level 8 is usually the home of an unwitting victim who

had their eye focused too firmly on Level 7 (Apathy), but
ran out of the strength or will to hold that delicate balance. Younger employees will almost always fall back
into a series of 3-6 Loops (Chapter 11 – Cyclic Trends)
or choose to hide out in Level 2 (Nodding and Agreeing),
Level 4 (Escape), or one of the self-maintaining Trends
(see Chapter 12).

Level 8's who have gone beyond the vocational point-
of-no-return need an ". . . it's only a job" wake-up call.
Nothing is worth sacrificing your health and reducing
your lifespan over. Give yourself a break; you didn't plan
to end up here, it's not your fault, now move on and
have some fun!

Management Perspective

As a manager of a Level 8, your goal is exactly the
same as what I just told the employee. Help him/her to
face reality, get healthy, and get on with the rest of their
life. Level 8 (Decline and Surrender) is just that, a slow,
unstoppable decline based on being too weak to keep
fighting.

You are not being disrespectful or unfair in doing
whatever it takes to help this person get the best retirement package possible and get on with planning the rest
of their life. You are doing the right thing for them, their
family, the company and your department. This is not
a place to pussy foot or beat around the bush. A Level
8 will never be a capable team player. They may be able
to offer some experienced council and valuable insights
before they go, so use the remaining time wisely to pick
their brain and let their talent and knowledge rub off on
other members of your staff, but do not be fooled into
thinking they will hold up under the pressure of the
real world.

The fragile few who actually make it to Level 8 are in
a place they never planned to be and, as their supervisor, the most therapeutic and caring thing you can do
is help them quickly through it. Look at it this way; the

faster they admit to the reality of their situation and move to make the most out of their remaining years, the better it will be for everyone.

If they are a long-term employee with political ties to the firm, be cognizant of that in working out an exit strategy, but remember: your number one goal is to make your department better, not to carry people who can't keep up. Don't be rude or hurtful, as this person is deserving of your respect for their long and dedicated service. Handle it, do what's right, then get back to reeling in your Level 3's (Griping and Complaining), 5's (Gut Check), 6's (Class Clown) and as many 4's (Escape) as you can.

Chapter 9
Level 9 – Paranoia

Level 9 is to Level 8 (Decline and Surrender) as Level 6 (Class Clown) is to Level 5 (Gut Check) – a break from the discomfort for a while, in a warped sort of way. This is where serious mental illness (we all have casual mental illness) enters the picture and with it certain concerns as to the safety of others. Most Level 9's are either very happy or very sad, and can quickly fluctuate between the two. Their eyes wander while they are talking and they frequently forget words or subjects.

Level 9's are to the point where they actually consider alternatives for permanent escape (see Level 10). Professional help is the best you can recommend to your Level 9 friends or subordinates, however don't expect them to jump at the suggestion.

Level 9 symptoms include:

- Uncontrollable laughing or sometimes even crying
- Lack of concentration
- Very low self esteem
- Willingness to jump on bandwagons

Although Level 9's may gather in Level 3 "bellyache brotherhoods" on occasion, they are not emotionally stable enough to maintain a rational conversation without either threatening someone or breaking down into a quivering mass. They normally travel in pairs and use each other's warped impressions of reality to justify their own.

... Old School Joe and Beloved Betty

Betty and Joe came from the old school. Shipping & Receiving was a small and easily managed department back then, and Betty was a wizard at coordinating incoming inspections and scheduling product shipments to a growing number of locations. When she started back in 1974, it was a manual task, using handwritten charts and large, wall-sized calendars to plan shipping deadlines and materials receipts. As the size of the department, the complexity of the operations, and the use of computer technology grew, Betty began to experience more stress and pressure with her expanding job responsibilities. Like most of her counterparts, she could sometimes be found participating in Level 3 "fret frats" during breaks and at lunchtime. It was a harmless way of purging some of the day's frustration and actually became kind of fun, reeling in an occasional Level 6 (Class Clown) or two.

Like many regularly enjoyed pastimes, however, whining and moaning soon began to be a habit for

Betty. She didn't realize that it was slowly undermining her normally positive attitude. What was a simple form of ventilation therapy that posed no real harm was now becoming a part of her personality below her conscious awareness. It wasn't going unnoticed by others in her department, however.

Joe and Betty became friends through their involvement in the lunchtime ritual of venting their unhappiness about various aspects of their work. Joe was the foreman over the Tool Crib and could match every one of Betty's shipping nightmares with a similar experience transpiring around some lost or broken piece of tooling or missing grinding wheel. As with negative habit patterns that revolve around the " . . . you're not going to believe this one . . . " type of stories, the two started to feed off each other. They began to take their casual membership in various "carp clusters" to new heights of proficiency that they found gratifying. Others soon began to distance themselves from this group, though, as it became more serious and less just simple fun.

Before long, Betty and Joe were actually getting more power and exhilaration from their shared paranoia during story times than from their actual jobs. This phenomenon allowed them to continue to perform their jobs proficiently, while avoiding most of the Level 4 (Escape), 5 (Gut Check) and 6 (Class Clown) symptoms that many of their peers were experiencing.

There is certainly nothing wrong with missing out on several of the most debilitating levels during your career. Unfortunately, Level 9 (Paranoia) becomes a box canyon, much like Level 2 (Nodding and Agreeing) or Level 4 (Escape). It provides a rush and some strength to carry on, but becomes its own self-maintaining trend. After years of practice, the advanced Level 9 becomes skilled at "making mountains out of mole hills" and develops a paranoid fear and an overly emotional view of everything that is going on. They need the fix of dwelling on and expanding the influence of events and experiences during their work day, very much like the Level 4 needs that one more beer at last call.

Because they began this habit pattern as a positive way to alleviate growing frustration, and initially it worked, most Level 9's do not see the subtle changes in their motives until they are finally pointed out by a concerned coworker. Only the most well-meaning friends will even offer this advice, and when they do, it will usually be met by immediate denial and defensiveness, much like the alcoholic defends his or her "social drinking."

Level 9's can be very destructive to an organization, because they are often people who were initially respected by a wide range of other employees. Since they feed on each other and develop an emotional need for the stimulus of the game, their numbers can grow geometrically, once they get a foothold. It is very easy for other employees with frustrations on their minds to be absorbed into these negative groups, which lowers the morale of a widening circle of influence.

It takes a long time for Level 9 status to reach a dangerous stage, so management should be on the lookout and attempt to catch and neutralize these behaviors early. The only solution for a serious, terminal case may be to strongly suggest exercising an early retirement option or intimating an unfavorable transfer.

Employee Perspective

Every company has a small number of Level 9's floating around, but I doubt if many will be reading this book. If you're one, congratulations, you are already on the right track. Level 9 is where you end up if you survive or sneak around Level 8 (Decline and Surrender) and don't take the advice in the last chapter. Others of you simply skipped a bunch of levels, avoided getting in the "Cyclic Trends" (see Chapter 11) or the other "Self-Maintaining Trends" (see Chapter 12) and got here when the habit of negativity became your reason for living.

Good news, it's all in your head! I don't mean to make fun of the situation, but it's true. You are a "glass is half empty" person to the extreme. You need to either "get over it", get back to a more positive outlook and re-join the functional members of your department, or get the professional help you need to do it. There is nothing wrong with admitting to some mental challenges and getting the assistance of a good shrink (a real shrink, not someone like me who just plays one on TV) to get you back to a productive and happy life.

I can guarantee you that one of the first steps will be to change who you spend time with. Level 9's pair up and cry on each other's shoulder, so you need to break away or get your Level 9 friend(s) to get healed with you; not too likely. Definitely try it, but don't expect the members of your favorite "gripe group" to gleefully jump at the chance to go get their head shrunk with you. If it were that easy, you'd have done it already. This is a decision about you and it's your time to get it right. You have no idea how much you're missing with that dark cloud over your head all the time.

Management Perspective

Level 9 is a rather diverse group, so you need to do a little homework before dealing with them. While they are not hard to identify using the above symptoms, depend-ing on their age, sex, job level, and the others in their favorite "pout posse", you will find that there is no one right way to deal with them. The one universal truth is that they do not realize how much time and effort they put into "woe is me" – time that is being taken away from their job, and you're paying for it!

The best initial test question may be just that; con-front them with the truth, that they are wasting time on the company's dime, and see their reaction. If it gets them thinking, feeling a bit embarrassed, or apologetic, you might have a chance. If they get defensive and an-gry, you have a case where they will need help beyond what you are qualified to give.

Once again, these folks are not going to be easily

won back to the team, and during a time when you have good potential with your more malleable staffers, you can't afford to spend too much time guessing. If the person in question is a younger employee, they are worth some initial effort, assuming you get reaction #1, above. If they are older and "set in their ways" you should either leave them alone, as long as they are not bringing down the whole department, or get assistance from upper management.

You do not want to fight with Level 9's, anger them, or make them into a bigger problem than they already are. Usually, low self esteem is a prerequisite for Level 9 issues, and that is something that you can do only so much to build up. Self esteem issues come from a very young age, as early as 4-6 years old, and are the result of poor parenting or negative involvement with other authority figures. Much of their issues are deeply subconscious and may require professional help, something well beyond the scope of a caring supervisor or friend.

My suggestion is to make a rapid diagnosis, then get the help you need to keep your Level 9's from infecting the rest of your people. This kind of negative, gossipy behavior is very contagious and can undermine a broad range of people quickly. Level 9's are to be separated, then dealt with as quickly as possible.

The Ten LEVELS
DISBELIEF 1
NODDING & AGREEING 2
GRIPING & COMPLAINING 3
ESCAPE 4
GUT CHECK 5
6 CLASS CLOWN
7 APATHY
8 SURRENDER
10 INSANITY

Chapter 10
Level 10 – Insanity

The final level is pretty self-explanatory. When all other attempts have been exhausted, an individual will succumb to "Workplace Insanity." Psychologists tell us we all have a pre-chosen escape route in our subconscious mind should we ever need it, so this level is an automatic final step, when all else fails.

There are no symptoms of Level 10, because by the time someone chooses this level, it is too late to diagnose. Hopefully, a Level 10 will not harm themselves or others in carrying out their decision, but this is an area in which much is theorized, yet nothing is consistent enough to anticipate. Only a very small percentage of our nation's employee base ever approaches Level 10, and an even smaller percentage actually follows through. While that is reassuring, it is still well advised to have some understanding of the subtle characteristics that may lead to this level.

... this is "love-my-job" Earl

Earl was one of those guys whose whole life revolved around his work. Everyone knew that he would never retire, but hoped he would find some other interests outside the office. Ever since that nasty divorce back in 1992, he has buried himself in his work to overcome the pain and loneliness. He doesn't *seem* sad or lonely, and his work of negotiating large projects for the Corporate Special Projects department is unparalleled in the company. Earl is a pillar of the community and a positive spokesman for the company in social settings and in dealings with both customers and vendors. This is the last guy who people would wonder about, unless they really got to know him.

Earl's ability to hold his emotions well in check has made it difficult to categorize him in the *Ten Levels of Workplace Disillusionment* for any length of time. When things get tough, he seems to be able to take a deep breath and move on unabashed. While this certainly has been beneficial in his ability to work well with others and achieve multiple promotions during his 26-year career, the internal effects went unnoticed for a long time. When they finally reared their ugly head, Earl's symptoms were vague and inconsistent. Bouts of forgetfulness, periods of quiet "insanity" where he seemed to be in another world, uncharacteristic anger at what were normally "no big deal" issues for him. His peers and subordinates at first just shrugged these episodes off under the heading of "everybody has a bad day now and then."

Because of his internal focus, and ability to keep problems bottled up inside, he never outwardly demonstrated any of the common Level 3, Level 5, or Level 8 symptoms of frustration or resentment that many of the other employees experienced as they climbed the corporate ladder. He probably did go through these levels, but was able to masterfully hide them from those around who had too many of their own problems to deal with to question the unshared issues of Earl, who always appeared to have it all together.

When they finally came and hauled Earl off, it was a shock to everybody in his department. All of life's pressures finally added up and overcame Earl's ability to hold them at bay. Fortunately, Earl did not do damage to himself or others, but in other Level 10 situations it could have been drastically different. A very small percentage of the American workforce experiences Level 10, so it is difficult for management to either anticipate or react to warning signs. Obviously, the Type A workaholic, with minimal outside interests, is a possible indication. However, it is really nobody's business what employees do with their personal time, so it is not always easy to determine when, or if, to step in.

Because of its very limited application and indistinguishable symptoms, Level 10 is one of those unavoidable statistics that will plague many companies from time to time. Management's goal (hopefully) of identifying negative behavior patterns, confronting them in cooperation with the employee, and implementing new options for a healthier work experience may serve to catch potential Level 10 candidates long before they reach a point where Level 10 is a viable life option.

Employee Perspective

If you were actually a Level 10 you would not be reading this silly book, so I'm going to talk to you as if you were not yet there, just kicking the tires. Don't do it, man! You are either a Level 8 (Decline & Surrender), or Level 9 (Paranoia), so the first thing to do is go back and reread the last two chapters. My advice to you would be similar to a Level 8, get life in perspective. If your job is really making you nuts, it isn't worth it. Get some help, train for a marathon, change your hobbies, make a change.

Level 10 is a very rare level and the folks who get here usually do it fast and without warning. Some do damage to themselves, sometimes to others, and in some cases both. Either way you don't come back from it, so don't take the chance. You're not a Level 10, now go get the help you need!

Management Perspective

Good news; you may never have to deal with a Level 10 during your entire career. Better news; if you do, it will be something you have no warning about, or control over, so you won't be at fault. Bad news; it's never pretty. "Workplace Insanity" is just that – insane, so you can't anticipate it, fix it, understand it or correct it.

It's some kind of a meltdown, and there's rarely a ready disaster plan. Fallout can include a gap in your team and a domino effect of "down time." Your job is to protect the rest of your people from it. It is rare and over fast, so I wouldn't worry too much about Level 10 readiness. Let's wrap up Part Two and get on to some other tools and understandings that will help you with the heart and soul of your department, not dwell on the few, rare exceptions.

Summation

The majority of employees who enter the *Ten Levels* slip relatively quickly through Level 1 (Disbelief) and Level 2 (Nodding and Agreeing). Fortunately, not very many travel through Levels 8 (Decline and Surrender), 9 (Paranoia) and 10 (Insanity) during their career. Most of those who remain stuck within the *Ten Levels* get out at or before Level 8 through retirement, disability, or premature death.

The majority of us bounce around between Level 3 (Griping and Complaining) and Level 6 (Class Clown). The next largest group hides out in Level 4 (Escape), with a smaller percentage settling for Level 2 (Nodding and Agreeing) and Level 9 (Paranoia). A few are able to balance on Level 7 (Apathy) until they retire. The lucky ones get out of the game altogether and take on a whole other array of challenges by either working in a more motivating, less political job, or by starting their own businesses.

It has taken 20 years of tinkering and fine tuning to get the *Ten Levels* to where they are today. They are now the definitive building blocks of workplace dysfunction and, in that sense, provide a track to run on in evaluating the morale, productivity, performance, teamwork and hidden potential of any workplace, in any industry. Each level is an exercise in realizing and understanding the power of habit and how it hooks people out of desperation, discomfort or convenience into ways of handling the day-to-day stress of work.

Over the years, I've been amazed at the way different personality types tended to follow each other like lemmings into the same cycles or traps, often wasting vast portions of their working life. After more intensely observing and researching from the sidelines for the last few years, it was time to jump back in with some observations, suggestions and a helpful tool to get everybody to look honestly at their way of living at work and together pulling each other out of the quicksand.

While we have spent a lot of time delving into the

Ten Levels, this is really a four-part book with the ultimate goal of helping everyone out of the prison that a work life within the levels represents. Part One introduces the premise behind the study of the *Ten Levels*. Part Two is like basic math – you get each principle one at a time and need to develop a proficiency in working with them before you are ready to use them in equations.

Part Three is the Algebra; viewing the levels as they react and intertwine with each other like recurring equations of life. This is where you will get a true feel for where you stand and, hopefully, gain confidence to help you and your coworkers get out of the cycle.

Part Four is the Calculus, where the rubber meets the road; the real-world applications that make studying the fundamentals pay off. Getting off of the Merry-Go-Round is what this book is all about. Fortunately, I have done it and have some great tools to share that can help you and your fellow employees do it too.

Employee Perspective

I studied the *Ten Levels* from the inside during my early years in the corporate workforce, then for 15 more years from the other side, as a recognition consultant to the managerial side, so I have had the benefit of molding my views about the levels from multiple perspectives over a long period of time. Part Three, coming up, is the meat and potatoes of this book, so I strongly suggest you get yourself as familiar as possible with the *Ten Levels*, and get a feel for them. It will make it easier to appreciate the subtleties of the Trends in the next two chapters.

A good working knowledge of the *Ten Levels* will also help you in dealing with your coworkers. You will have the advantage of paying attention to the behaviors, the dialogue, and the reactions of other people as they interact, rather than missing portions while you strive to remember which level symptoms they are exhibiting. Hey, it's only Ten – memorize it! Just humor me for now! You'll thank me after Chapter 13.

Management Perspective

Instructing your employees on the dynamics of the *Ten Levels of Workplace Disillusionment* can result in a happier, more productive staff. Your thorough knowledge of the *Ten Levels* and the Trends will make this process more rewarding, because you may find that you exhibit some of these reactionary tendencies and must deal with them before you can lead your team in overcoming theirs.

As a trainer, motivator and coach to your employees, the knowledge you both have of the *Ten Levels* will give you some excellent tools to use in working to improve all aspects of workplace activity. I may be a little bit biased towards my version of why people do what they do at work, but in reality any tool that gets you and your workers singing from the same hymn book will give you the opportunity to generate fresh enthusiasm for the many ways whereby work can be more enjoyable and productive for all of you.

There is, however, a risk in helping your employees confront and deal with the causes or negative behavior patterns that affect them – you may be giving them the inner strength and confidence they need to leave your firm and go on to other greener pastures! While there is no denying the potential of this happening, the benefits if they stay are the seeds of a better working environment that will sprout up and intertwine with all your other employees now and in the future. In the same vein as tuition reimbursement and other work-related training, the improvements in the people you keep will far outweigh the loss of the ones who inevitably leave.

Part Three
Some Common Trends

Although everyone has a favorite level where they find comfort or justification for their discomfort, nobody stays in any one level all of the time. Some of your wimpiest Level 2's (Nodding and Agreeing), the most strung-out Level 4's (Escape), and the most resolute Level 9's (Paranoia) appear to be stuck there, but they all started out at Level 1 (Disbelief) and can get coaxed into other levels from time to time, even though they may hide it from the rest of us. Interaction with other people and job-related or personal challenges also work to alter our levels regularly. Close scrutiny has distinguished some trends in the way many of us slide up and down the chart.

Two types of trends exist throughout the *Ten Levels of Workplace Disillusionment*. I call them "Cyclic Trends" and "Self-Maintaining Trends."

Chapter 11
Cyclic Trends

The 3-6 Loop

The 3-6 Loop is the most noteworthy cyclic trend besetting professionals in project-oriented positions. I was a big time "3-6 Looper" as an Industrial Engineer in my first two jobs after college. The jump from Level 1 (Disbelief) to 2 (Nodding and Agreeing), for most new employees, is quite rapid. The jump from Level 2 to Level 3 (Griping and Complaining) is even faster. This represents the "look out world, here I come" attitude that many college grads bring to their first jobs, because they have a lot of knowledge, ego and naivety, but no understanding of corporate politics.

Due to the stress and confusion associated with re-siding in Level 3 and constantly trying to find a valuable contribution to make, Level 4 (Escape) and Level 5 (Gut Check) inevitably become considerations. The self-motivated achiever will normally not be lured into Level 4, at least the first few times around the loop. Level 5, however, is ready and waiting for the "go-getter" who enthusiastically bounds over Level 4 toward success.

The tricky part of Level 5 (Gut Check) is that it creeps up subtly and isn't noticeable to others. Add to that the fact that it often affects younger employees who feel invincible at this stage of life and may be putting in some long, dedicated hours at the expense of proper diet and exercise, which results in a person ripe for internal complications. The struggling achiever seems to be func-tioning normally while he or she is actually experiencing unfamiliar internal annoyances.

I don't know about you, but I have found intestinal pain to be very difficult to endure for a long period of time. This tends to explain the transference to Level 6 (Class Clown) for a reprieve. It also can lead to some explanation of why a perfectly normal, hardworking employee can suddenly fall into Level 4 after a few laps around the 3-6 Loop. Level 6 inhabitants are very congenial and light hearted. I venture to say that many of your office's "good time Charlies" are Level 6 aficionados. Although borderline loony, the Level 6 sojourner is often just taking a breather from his fast-paced success plan to have some fun. The longer an individual fights to stay out of Level 5, the more likely they are to experience the more severe peculiarities of Level 6, when he or she finally succumbs to goofing off. Sometimes, though, the medications taken to survive prolonged stays in Level 5, or the innocent couple of beers after work, can slowly begin to make our valuable contributor a candidate for Level 4 rather than Level 6 the next time around the loop. What makes it so dangerous is that, like Level 5, Level 4 is not a planned escape for the high achiever. It just starts to develop into a habit pattern of socially acceptable stress relief and then escalates from there.

Level 7 (Apathy) is an island. It is a turning point incomprehensible to the young achiever, because apathy at this stage in his or her career is not an option. Visualizing Level 7 only creates anger and aggravation, because it is like quitting. So where do you go after mellowing out in Level 6 (Class Clown) for a while? There are three options:

- Back to Level 3 (Griping and Complaining), when the next fresh challenge comes your way, to begin another trip around the 3-6 Loop.

- On to Level 7 (Apathy), for the attempt to maintain a noncommittal position towards work, until retirement, without experiencing significant guilt feelings.

- Break free from the cycle by joining with a group of fellow employees who support each other and have common goals, or by starting your own business outside the restrictions of corporate politics.

Frankly, the third, and most obvious, choice is usually not selected. This is due to fear and ego conflicts we all possess, and because tools like *The Vocational Shrink* have not been available to offer a believable alternative. Many of our country's best-run companies are beginning to make option three groups available to their employees to avoid losing them to the system, independent business opportunities, or competitors that concentrate more on employee fulfillment programs.

I didn't have these options when I got out of school, so I ran the 3-6 Loop a bunch of times, learned all about self employment the hard way, and finally wrote this book. One of my goals is to save some people from traveling the whole, lonely path to fulfillment by themselves, as so many before them have tried to do. We can only guess how many people who stayed in the system until it was too late could have been helped if this book had been around sooner. I plan to make up for all those lost souls, by helping everyone I can now.

Better yet, perhaps I can have some impact on helping supervisors improve the quality of the workplace. When both employees and their managers are cognizant of, and have a desire to improve, the situation, the need to hole up in negative behavior levels and trends diminishes.

> When both employees and their managers are cognizant of and have a desire to improve the situation, the need to hole up in negative behavior levels and trends diminishes.

Even with change beginning to happen in the understanding of employee recognition, motivation and fulfillment, the plight of many of our society's young, aggressive achievers is to run the 3-6 Loop over and over until they finally exit through the ever-present temptation of Level 4 (Escape), the self-defeatist attitude of Level 9 (Paranoia), or the elusive nirvana of Level 7 (Apathy).

The Fulcrum – Level 7

The notable break in the *Ten Levels of Workplace Disillusionment* falls between Level 6 (Class Clown) and Level 7 (Apathy). There are a lot of "pseudo 7's" around, but the trained eye can discern them as "3-6 Loopers" experiencing another Level 6 delusion of grandeur. True Level 7's have made the choice to stay where they are forever (or at least until pending retirement). They don't want to make any waves or upset their routine, ". . . just leave me alone, I retire in 4 years, 3 months, 6 days, and 3 ½ hours." The problem with most Level 7's is that they were in the 3-6 Loop for years and the idea of just jumping off at the top of the pendulum, so to speak, is very foreign to their character and lifelong habits. They are fed up with the 3-6 Loop, but scared to death of dropping over the top into Levels 8, 9 or 10. The longer they wait to take on the Fulcrum, though, the less chance they will have to balance it effectively. It is a "Catch 22" between conserving enough energy to maintain a balance on the Fulcrum, and waiting until they are close enough to retirement to kick into their final sprint. This need for such precise timing is why it is so difficult to pull off a true Level 7 experience.

When someone who is used to being frustrated and challenged every day decides to try something different, but realizes they are too old and out of vocational shape to change careers, the immediate sensation is one of relief. The long-term result, however, may be a slow slide into self-pity, and a realization of old age setting in. By definition, apathy assumes you are of no real value other than in your high level of skill at ducking at all the right times and avoiding any kind of responsibility . . . hello, Level 8 (Decline and Surrender)!

Unfortunately, once Level 8 symptoms begin to appear there is usually no turning back. The body and mind begin the slow process of degeneration, often followed by retirement and an early demise. That's why even the few apparent Level 7 (Apathy) success stories don't often end up in successful, energetic, long-lasting retirement experiences. The habit is simply too hard to break, and any Level 8 symptoms that did begin only make it harder.

Well, so much for the oasis of Level 7. Staying on the Fulcrum as the pendulum swings back to Level 3 (Griping and Complaining) and over to Level 8 is extremely difficult and taxing on the system (sounds a little like Level 3, again, doesn't it?). The only way I've seen someone remain in Level 7 is to keep so actively involved in outside activities that they can put in their hours at work and not get into the internal politics. It translates into bringing the body to work and leaving the mind at home, and that is the ultimate waste for both the company and the employee.

Go directly to
your cubicle.

Do not pass Go.

Do not
collect $200.

Chapter 12
Self-Maintaining Trends

The Trap – Level 2

People who dwell in Level 2 (Nodding and Agreeing) for very long are candidates for the Trap. Individuals with low self-esteem, inadequate or outdated skills and limited drive can easily find ways to justify permanent residence in Level 2. Fear and lack of self respect, combined with "Peter Principle" (see Chapter 2, Level 2 Nodding and Agreeing) incompetence, is the recipe for the Trap. Although most of us would be uncomfortable  "sucking up" all the time, the knowledge that they are in a position and a salary range far greater than they could achieve anywhere else creates a comfort zone, in a warped sense of the word.

"Trappers" can be very bad for a company, because they will agree with the boss no matter what he or she says. At best, this affords no creative input or help to the company's leaders. At worst, it can give the boss a false sense of capability that may lead to costly mistakes in judgment, and inefficient utilization of company resources.

It is poor stewardship on the company's part to allow employees to flounder aimlessly on the payroll. If the boss believes that he can do everything himself, without the help of real experts (his Level 2 "experts" are a sham), the company suffers and is at risk of being overtaken by better-managed competition.

There is a lot of guilt associated with Level 2, either by the employee who misuses his or her position or by the employer who allows it to happen, or both. In the situations I have witnessed, the worst Level 2's are there as a favor to pay a past business debt and are simply too selfish to bow out gracefully and rejoin the functional world. They are content to carry a prestigious title, rake in the paycheck, the benefits and the perks. These people are few, in this day and age, but astute management and common sense go a long way toward recognizing and eradicating the company of this negative situation. Level 2's are quickly identified and eliminated in a family business when competent, professional management is brought in and the "good ol' boy" network loses power. Unfortunately, this often takes the death of the founding entrepreneur who would never seek retirement and cannot be easily forced out.

The Escape – Level 4

Escape from the struggles of day-to-day life (drugs, alcohol, gambling and other addictions) is common practice for many people. The problem, as with most habits, occurs when socially acceptable, voluntary es-

cape becomes a necessary activity no longer controllable by the user. The option to move from the stresses of Level 3 (Griping and Complaining) to the perceived contentment of Level 4 (Escape) can be pretty tough to resist, making it the easiest out available for many. Add to that how easy it is for that innocent couple of beers after work to become a needed fix, or those few pills taken from time to time (usually for hidden Level 5 symptoms) to become a daily ritual, and you can see why bars and casinos are so busy.

The Escape victim is the person who lacks the self-discipline and peer support to use chemicals in moderation or not at all. As in the Trap, he or she finds ways to justify remaining in an unhealthy state. The rationale is based on a subconscious dependence on the drugs (they could never consciously admit to an addiction) rather than on fear and incompetence, as with Level 2 (Nodding and Agreeing). A lack of self-confidence and its associated anxiety can contribute to a person's involvement in the Escape, but the continued use of chemicals to relieve frustration affects the mind's ability to generate rational thought patterns – and rational thought patterns are the only way out. Level 4 is characterized by a worsening spiral, a true self-destructive, self-maintaining trend.

The Whiner – Level 9

What starts out as innocent banter about the daily frustrations of the work day can ultimately lead to an almost addictive need for a regular dose of complaining. Level 3's (Griping and Complaining) sometimes get so into the antics of their favorite "remonstration organization" that it becomes their "drug" of choice. When this happens, they will team up with another one or two people with a similar weakness and literally feed off of each other's negativism. While this goes unnoticed within the group, they start to be seen as chronic complainers, and that really turns off those "glass is half full" producers that you value so much in your organization.

It is important for management to identify, isolate and individually work with these people to wean them from this habit. If it is caught and brought to their attention early enough, Whiners may be receptive to the corrective criticism and realize that they have gotten a little carried away with the extent and vociferousness of their impatience with company systems and procedures. You may be able to make them a part of the solution, rather than allowing them to remain a part of the problem, and bring them back to a position where they are productive and positive again. They may still be prime candidates for normal Level 3 behavior, but hopefully will be cognizant of the point where healthy discussions begin to turn into overreactions, and will know when to quit.

If you get to them too late for a healthy turnaround, you are left to deal with them as you would a Level 2 (Nodding and Agreeing) or Level 4 (Escape). They need to be led to a realistic and low-visibility retirement or resignation option. The goal is to allow them to save face without getting into a battle of wits that can never be won, and which only serves to substantiate what everyone already knows.

Chapter 13
Hints to Identifying Levels

As an employee or supervisor, one of the greatest initial challenges of using the information in *The Vocational Shrink – An Analysis of the Ten Levels of Workplace Disillusionment* will be identifying levels. When implementing the Game into your workplace, the ability to quickly and accurately identify the various levels you and your fellow workers are using on a day-to-day basis is the key to progress and a continued effort by all parties.

One of the best ways to do this is to ask a question. Depending on the answer, you will often be able to quickly identify their current level and begin to work through the process of determining the personality characteristics, habit patterns and stimuli that are causing the negative reaction. Remember, for this to work it needs to be honest, empathetic, fun and non-threatening. Only revelations thoroughly embraced by an employee have any hope of being acted upon. Here are a few examples:

1. Ask a committing question, such as:
   "How do you think we ought to do such and such?"

A **Level 1** will – sigh, roll their eyes or look upwards, and deliberate over the response that will make them look most like a team player.

A **Level 2** will – talk around the question and try to change the subject to a non-business related area. Or, he might become angry and refuse to respond, using some excuse as to the validity of the question based on your job description.

A **Level 3** will – offer two or three solutions and volunteer to spearhead the project.

Level 4 will – probably misunderstand the question or

attempt to show why it doesn't involve him or her.

A **Level 5** will – smile, wince, excuse themselves, and hurry off towards the facilities. Or, they'll respond much like a Level 3, then smile, wince, excuse themselves and hurry off towards the facilities.

A **Level 6** will – be reminded of a joke.

A **Level 7** will – chuckle, and then slowly respond with a blue-sky solution that would never fly within the existing budget structure.

[Don't ask questions of Level 8's, 9's and 10's!]

---

2. Compliment the person in a personal, non-performance related area, such as:
"That's a sharp-looking new car, Joyce."

A **Level 1** will – smile big, thank you a little more than you feel the compliment is due, and try to make friends. He or she will probably ask a company policy-related question, if you react positively to their gesture.

A **Level 2** will – deny the validity of the gesture and wonder what you want them to do (a step backwards, wringing of hands, and/or a nervous grin may accompany the comment).

A **Level 3** will – tell you the complete history of the particular model and manufacturer and then expound on how to get a good deal on one.

A **Level 4** will – probably misunderstand the comment or attempt to show why it doesn't involve them.

A **Level 5** will – thank you graciously, then smile, wince, excuse themselves and hurry off towards the facilities.

A **Level 6** will – laugh, make a joke about the car, and

then break into an impression of a coworker stuck in traffic.

A **Level 7** will – be taken aback at the idea that some-one would extend a positive observation their way, then slowly recount the story of their first car and how fun it was to drive it in the country with the top down.

//
3. Ask a question about personal goals, like:
"Where do you see yourself in three years, Bruce?"

A **Level 1** will – sigh, seriously consider the question, and then respond with a canned answer they think you want to hear.

A **Level 2** will – feel threatened, beat around the bush, avoid the question, become uncomfortable about his or her privacy being invaded (they know they'll be doing exactly the same thing in three years, barring a major upper management change).

A **Level 3** will – mention several "fast lane" ideas and describe the people, places, and specific short- and long-term goals involved in the plan.

A **Level 4** will – probably misunderstand the question or attempt to show why it doesn't involve him or her.

A **Level 5** will – get initially enthusiastic about goals and dreams, then smile, wince, excuse themselves and hurry off towards the facilities.

A **Level 6** will – laugh, say something strange like "a tightrope walker with Barnum and Bailey", then begin humming the circus theme like a calliope.

A **Level 7** will – chuckle, and go into excruciating detail about his hideaway in the mountains with the babbling brook, and the animals, and the peace, and the serenity . . .

These are just a few examples, but they demonstrate how easy it is to design questions relevant to your business and workforce that will quickly identify and categorize your people in a simple and non-confrontive manner.

Summation

Understanding the way the *Ten Levels* fit into trends is helpful in predicting how different personality types will vacillate between levels during their work lives. As trends develop, the habits that control the choices which lead to reactive options become grouped in a repeatable series. Elimination of the control and time lost to the *Ten Levels* becomes more and more difficult as people unknowingly fall into the clutches of various behavioral trends.

The problem is rooted in the very way our minds are built to work. The subconscious mind always provides what it thinks we want out of life based on all the information we've put in since we were born. Most of our decisions every day are subconsciously generated from deep-seated beliefs stored in the subconscious, so they occur without thought or question. The first step in changing behavior is the awareness of our habits, and then using our current levels of information and logic to reconsider the actions.

One of my favorite Star Trek episodes, "Shore Leave" (Season 1, Episode 15 for you Trekies), is the one where the crew of the Enterprise lands on a recreational planet for some R&R. Captain Kirk ends up meeting a rival from his academy days and they fight just like old times while Mr. Sulu is attacked by a Samurai Warrior and must fight to the death. Each crew member confronts one of their hidden demons that was locked up deep in their mind, until the advanced race that runs the planet realizes that the primitive Earth people are not mentally sophisticated enough to use his planet as it was designed.

This recreational facility allows each guest to create any experience in their mind to enjoy as if it were real.

Unfortunately, these lowly humans allowed negative thoughts to enter their heads and the planet, much like our own subconscious mind, simply created these realities, without questioning whether or not they were right. Sadly, many people go through their whole lives allowing negative, scary, self-limiting thoughts to control their mind, and their subconscious dutifully makes sure that their desires are found in the world around them.

This is the most profound and powerful revelation I can share with you, and it's a major key to why some people are far more successful, capable and happy than other people. It's not brains, talent or luck that makes the difference. Rather, it's what we believe and expect from ourselves that determines how far we can go. The use of *The Vocational Shrink* in an unintimidating and supportive atmosphere could lead to a healthy realization of time spent in various levels and trends. This simple act of bringing subconscious behavior patterns into the conscious mind will provide an opportunity to consider how new habits can forge a far happier, healthier and profitable work environment.

> It's not brains, talent, or luck that makes the difference. Rather, it's what we believe and expect from ourselves that determines how far we can go.

For all of you who read the last page of a book first, peek at the results of the *Motor Trend* new car comparisons before reading the article, or just plain visualize a short cut in everything – surprise!

Part Four
Using the
Ten Levels to Make Changes

The previous 13 chapters represent the first step to getting off the merry-go-round. So, if you haven't read them yet, nice try. Go back to the beginning!

Chapter 14
How to Get Off the Merry-go-round

Believe it or not, this part is simple (not easy, but simple). Actually, getting off the merry-go-round is a lot easier than the games we all go through scampering up and down the *Ten Levels* year after year. There are three steps to counteracting a life of habitual frustration living within the *Ten Levels of Workplace Disillusionment*, or to changing any habit for that matter. Before looking at the steps to changing habits, let's discuss how habits are developed and how dominating they are to our lives.

Habits are reactions that we choose, without conscious thought, based on programming that has been entered into our subconscious minds throughout our lives. The human subconscious mind works similar to a computer. It takes in stimulus and outputs what it thinks we want based on the beliefs that we have stored in our memory banks. It does this automatically, all the time.

Our subconscious does not distinguish between positive and negative input, it simply gives us what the input appears to represent based on this extensive library of beliefs, fears and predetermined responses. Each of our libraries includes all the things that have happened to us and been told to us by parents, teachers, friends, heroes – anyone seen as an authority figure – not necessarily an authority figure now, but when the experience happened to us! A person may have been an authority figure when we were young because we feared them, not because they were smart or right. Perhaps older children had a profound influence on us, including bullies and con artists. A belief does not have to be valid to control our future decision-making, only believed. That is why it is important to evaluate all questionable past beliefs from a current, adult perspective and decide if they are valuable to our life today.

Here's an example. Remember the last time you were with a group and saw a snake or lizard? Some people may have wanted to touch or hold it, while others ran for cover. The same stimulus yields completely different, totally subconscious reactions in that instant, affecting each person without thought. They probably didn't calmly whip out their trusty trail guide to identify the species and determine if it was poisonous, then decide if it was safe to approach. No, most people have a pre-programmed reaction to reptiles that elicits an immediate reaction based on some earlier (perhaps much earlier) situation, and that decision has never since been questioned.

More than 90 percent of the things we do each day are controlled by this same kind of response. These are based on feelings, fears, beliefs – ultimately decisions, made by the time we were five or six years old. Think about that for a minute. Almost every response we have to what goes on around us is controlled subconsciously by habits that were formed from events affecting us made as a young child.

The first step to all self-improvement is self-evaluation of our beliefs and the habits we've formed based on those beliefs. That means we must begin to think about the reactions we have to every stimulus that comes our way and consciously determine if the reaction we have, or the action we take, is the one we really want. Is it still valid today, considering what I know to be true? Is it moving me ahead or holding me back? Is it a well-thought-out, realistic response, or a habitual reaction based on old information that is not best for my life today? If you are like me, this process will be surprising, and quite embarrassing in many cases. But until we begin to identify and question our habitual reactions to life, we will be limited in seeing how our movement within the *Ten Levels* can be interpreted.

While I'd suggest that our objective should be to become aware of our habit patterns in general, it's common that people prefer to stay with problems they understand, rather than look for solutions that make them uncomfortable. It is also true, however, that people do not really decide their future, they decide their habits. And then their habits decide their future . . .

Now that you have a real interest and a burning desire to evaluate and modify some reactionary behaviors, let's look at the three steps to changing any habit: awareness, support and practice.

Awareness

Ever notice how when we tell someone something about themselves they will tend to doubt or justify it, but if it's an idea they think of, it's true? Until you bring your actions into your conscious mind for evaluation based on your current knowledge and experience, it's doubtful you will ever change a behavior. You have to do this yourself. Any life change requires a personal desire to change. The reason you don't have that desire now is because the current habit is authorized by a subconscious belief that is never questioned. Once you bring it out on the table and look at it through today's eyes, you will see that – while it was an appropriate response at some time in your life – it may not be the best choice any longer.

Transactional Analysis is a theory that defines three

areas of the human mind: The Parent, The Adult and The Child. The Parent is the part of the brain that holds all of the rules and regulations that you received from parents, teachers and other authority figures during your upbringing. Some are positive, some negative, and some outdated "old wives' tales", but they're rooted there for subconscious retrieval nonetheless. "You are the spitting image of your father", "You're never going to be as smart as your sister", "Don't run with a sharp object", etc. This part of your brain acts as the parent or guardian of your mind. The Nurturing Parent is the loving, caring, supportive side. The Critical Parent holds all the do's and don'ts.

The Child area of the mind is made up of the Rebellious Child (the prankster, risk taker, rebel) and the Spontaneous Child (the playful, fun-loving, dancing, singing, crazy, carefree, careless, lazy part of your brain). This portion of your personality never grows up; it has no willpower, no self control and no discipline. That's where your fun and wild side lives.

The Adult side is the logical, conscious, "here and now" part of your brain. It is able to think things through and make logical determinations based on all of the knowledge you have accumulated during your life. The Adult is also ready to add any new information you choose to go out and get, such as the information in this book. It is the grown-up, decisive, calculating, serious, Mr. Spock part of your brain. Your best life decisions will be made by the Adult, if the Parent and Child allow that to happen.

Awareness comes from the Adult. When you see things through your conscious mind, you have the opportunity to evaluate your behaviors, beliefs and habits. Then you can consider viable, realistic, beneficial changes without the burden of the subconscious clutter messing up the Parent or Child portions of your personality.

Uncorrupted awareness of what you do, why you do it, and whether it is relevant and optimal for your life today is the starting point for all meaningful change. As you can see, it is also the most misunderstood and misinterpreted of the three steps.

Support

Once you have a handle on what habits you want and need to change, it is very helpful to have the support of other people who are involved in the same self-evaluation. Why? Mainly, because the reasons that support old habits will be somewhat illogical and possibly embarrassing – not the topic you are going to want to discuss with your regular "moan mob" during lunch. As soon as you are serious about identifying and attacking weak, ineffective habits, you are going to find that you will be more comfortable with other people who are challenging themselves in the same way. Conversely, you may begin to see the topics of the old "carp crowd" as pretty shallow and unimportant. This is the successful theory behind all support groups, such as Alcoholics Anonymous.

The *Ten Levels of Workplace Disillusionment – The Game* was developed to provide one way for a group to support each other in the workplace. It offers the ability for an entire department to address its habits from an equal footing and work towards a common goal. The key is to make the journey fun, rewarding and worth the ride. Equal support makes this possible, whereas going it alone has proven to be ineffective in establishing major, permanent change in the workplace or in life. Old habits are comfy, and when an attempt at change starts to jeopardize that comfort, it's surprisingly easy to justify the old habit and slide right back into a warm, cozy, negative pattern again.

Using a common tool, management is also able to interact in the process, both as an overseer of employee progress and as another source of change that can keep the process up to speed. Rarely are workplace issues confined to the employees only. Management's own habits, outdated procedures, and lack of human relations expertise are often key factors in holding a company back.

Most of today's current management books encourage a culture where supervisors take on a more supportive role, allowing employees to exercise their personal creativity and to take responsibility for their work. The more that employees feel empowered to control their work life, the more of their natural creativity and discretionary effort (that extra performance they bring to the workplace that the company gets for free) comes pouring out.

The Game is one of many tools that managers can use to help employees take more responsibility for themselves, their workplace attitudes, their personal productivity, and to evaluate the way they interact with each other. The more you as a manager do to simply provide the tools and let the employees use them as they see fit, the more long-term benefit you will realize. It's the old "two heads are better than one" approach taken to the max, and it works like a charm.

Practice

Habits are formed by practice. That is how the old ones were formed, and any new habits will require the same repetitive practice to take root. Experts agree that if you consciously change the way you do something, and keep doing it differently for about 21 days, it will become a habit. Try this. Every morning (you may not know this yet, but it's true) you put your shoes on in the same order – right then left or left then right. Determine which way you do it habitually, then consciously change it to the other way. Place a little note in your closet or on the mirror to remind you when you are getting dressed. If you stay with it, in about 21 days you will begin to put your shoes on this new way without thinking about it. While that is a simplistic example, it is exactly how all skills become habits. Writer and philosopher Henry David Thoreau said, "Things do not change; we do."

Everything from improving your memory to learning a foreign language to altering workplace habits will only change through repetitive attempts to stay on a new, initially uncomfortable track. This is the reason that a support group and a well-defined track are so important. Remember that life habits took your whole life to become engrained. Give them some time to become redirected or you will quickly lose heart and give up.

Practicing new skills as a team with a common goal is considered to be the most effective way to achieve significant and long-lasting changes. As a manager, you are the conductor of your workplace orchestra. You're responsible for the content, the tempo, and ultimately the symphony that will come forth. *The Vocational Shrink – The Game* can help focus your department's practice, keep it in perspective and, most importantly, make it fun and unthreatening to the employees. After all, it is their tenacity, persistence, and desire to change that will make progress a reality.

"Things do not change; we do."

– Henry David Thoreau

Chapter 15
A Ray of Sunshine in the Storm

 Just when you were beginning to get a little overwhelmed and starting to wonder how all this can work for you and your company, here is that extra support I told you about earlier.

Because this book is part of a business approach, which includes a game for training and a seminar for inspiring a diverse workforce, I am using this chapter to introduce the benefits of accessing a Greater Consciousness in a general way. Spirituality is a personal experience and a narrow view of it might work against the effectiveness of *The Vocational Shrink – An Analysis of the Ten Levels of Workplace Disillusionment* if its message has the potential for being offensive to any of my readership. I am, however, including a more complete version of my personal spiritual journey in this book's Appendix, if you would care to read it and get a more thorough understanding of my personal views and opinions.

We are all born into this world without an instruction book. Our parents didn't get one in the "newborn kit" when they brought us home from the hospital, and there is no owner's manual passed on to us when we venture out on our own. No wonder the optimum use of mind and body eludes most of us for the majority of our lives. Not surprisingly, those step-by-step programs for self-improvement leave us confused and still uncertain.

Well, good news! Just like new computers, we actually *do* have an owner's manual – but it is inside of us and similar to the on-line help that's only accessible by clicking on the little question mark on the computer screen. This higher consciousness, super consciousness, collective consciousness or greater power is available to lead us through the fog toward the best, most rewarding use of our lives . . . if we simply access it and utilize it. Just when you need it most – a ray of light during the storm!

Do you believe in fate? How about the idea that the people, things, and opportunities you need for success will show up at just the right time in your life, if you are only open to them? I didn't always believe it, but during the same two years that I first struggled within the *Ten Levels of Workplace Disillusionment* to find a purpose and a value to my life, I was led to a new way of seeing things. This gift has changed my view of everything, of everybody, and of what life is really about.

I was young, impatient and, after several short-lived jobs out of college, began to wonder if I would ever find a meaningful work experience. I was trying hard to achieve, to move ahead, and to get things done. You see, that was my problem, I was trying too hard, but I didn't know it. Physical things, like hammering a nail, work better when you hit them harder. Mental things are just the opposite. It's when you relax, pull back, and allow other, bigger forces than yourself to help you take a crack at it that you start to see a path through the storm and a light at the end of the tunnel.

One of the managers at work was different from the rest. He was frustrated and harried with his work, just like the rest of us, but seemed to have a deeper inner peace that was rather intriguing. I began to spend time sharing my confusion with this new friend and less time with my usual "hate horde." There was something about this guy that was down to earth and simple, yet fresh and positive.

Before you start saying, "Okay, here comes the God thing, again", ask yourself one question. If you have fallen victim to any of the *Ten Levels* traps or cycles that I had so much fun describing for you earlier, is there any chance that you too are trying overly hard to "do it all" yourself? It doesn't matter what background, experience, or education you have, there is a human tendency toward self-sufficiency in our society to which we all cling most of the time. I don't know whether it's human nature, or the way our parents raised us, but most of us tend to have a deeply ingrained habit to "roll up our sleeves", "put our nose to the grindstone" and "try, try again". How about this one: "When the going gets tough, the tough get going!" These clichés, and others like them, promote a goal of unrealistic self-sufficiency. Our upbringing, our heroes, and our peers seem to have created a "grownup" within each of us that is, by nature, very self-reliant.

What I learned from my friend is that there is another course. It's not a certain denomination, cult group, social club or other assemblage grabbing for some crutch. No, what I learned was that there is a very simple, readily available, totally free relationship with God available and this provides each of us with the potential for a level of supreme consciousness. All you have to do is say, "I'm ready." This struck me as a different offer than I had ever heard regarding a relationship with God. It had no strings, and a real "what do I have to lose?" feel about it. If true, I thought, I'd be better off. If it wasn't, I knew I had done nothing but waste a little time.

I've been benefiting from having a personal relationship with God for about 20 years. It has led to some amazing accomplishments in my life, but at the same time required some of the greatest sacrifices and hardest work. It is said that God provides the nuts, but he doesn't crack them. What I've found that to mean is that He will bring you what you want in life, but He will do it by allowing you to go through circumstances, challenges, and situations where you must make sacrifices.

As your selfishness goes away, you will look back and see that He didn't really do it for you, but led you through the growth opportunity to do it yourself. Yes, He may have provided some special people that showed up just at the right time to offer support, funding, encouragement and a shoulder... But, you will find that it's only when you've become a person who can handle a new blessing – in the proper way – it will happen, and not before. These blessings may be financial, but may also come in the form of strength of character or opportunities to serve and grow, things you may find to be of even greater value. Indeed, you could begin to grow and benefit in many ways.

If it wasn't this way, we would all be like lottery winners. We'd read The Book, slap God in our pocket like a rabbit's foot, and then start rattling off all of our wishes: "I wanna big house, a fast car, an' a big pile o' money!" But how many lottery winners do you hear about whose life and relationships wind up worse after their big win than they were before? Quite a lot of them . . . maybe most of them. And it's all because they got the goodies before they were emotionally and mentally prepared to make good use of them.

The privilege of writing this book is just one more step in this exciting journey toward the abundant answer to my first naive prayer. I never thought about being a writer. What do I have to say that would interest anyone? Come to think of it, I never thought about making a living as a commission salesperson or entrepreneur when I was young, either, but now I wouldn't do anything else. Hmm . . . I wonder what self-limiting messages I had to hurdle over in getting to where I am today? Just imagine what I might accomplish with the rest of my life! This is just a glimpse of that "cup runneth over" stuff He promises. I know that if I keep humbly asking and learning from the opportunities and trials my Friend is putting before me, I will actually become all I can be. And like all of us, that is far more than I could ever have imagined with my limited vision and confidence at the start. Philosopher Arthur Schopenhauer reminded us way back in 1850 that, "Every man takes the limits of his own field of vision for the limits of the world."

Here's one additional bonus for you. Remember my friend from work who initially shared this spiritual wealth with me? Not only has his life continued to blossom beyond his wildest dreams, but imagine the satisfaction he gets knowing that his lifestyle attracted someone to this opportunity and gave me a chance to get on the right track. He doesn't even know about this book yet, but I'm sure he will be flattered and moved by what he thought was just some candid advice from the heart.

Now that you are charged up a little bit more about all the new resources easily available to you and there just for the asking, think about this: You will never leave where you are until you decide where you want to be. And you will probably not decide where you want to be until you develop the increased confidence that you can really get there. I am convinced that you can best get this new confidence through the support of people and forces outside of yourself, and that opening yourself up can begin to light the fires that are dormant within you right now.

Summation

My reason for writing *The Vocational Shrink – An Analysis of the Ten Levels of Workplace Disillusionment* was to give employees a tool to use for identifying aspects of their personality and habit patterns that lead them to react to the stresses of the workplace in unhealthy ways. Once that is done, they are free to either accept this as their lot in life, or begin to go through a process of systematically changing some of their habits and take steps to become less likely to fall back into the negative spiral that the *Ten Levels* represent.

The ultimate choice we all have to consider is whether to become more effective in our current job, find a more fulfilling one, or quit the corporate life and venture out on our own. "In spite of all the warnings, nothing happens until the status quo becomes more painful than change," says writer Laurence Johnson Peter. An awareness of the status quo, and the belief that a change is both possible and advantageous, will come as you address and overcome your old, instinctive habits.

As managers begin making the *Ten Levels* material available in a nurturing way to their employees, the benefits of growth and individual improvements in performance and job satisfaction will be seeded and nurtured within the company and can directly impact the bottom line. This is certainly not guaranteed, as we mentioned before, because new insights by one's workers will bring new levels of confidence to them . . . and awareness of other possibilities for personal fulfillment. Be prepared to deal with this likelihood – the perfectly normal tendency for employees to "look around" or seek a change of scenery – by proactively creating "cool" motivational opportunities and recognition programs within your firm that reward and incentify your employees for challenging themselves to develop new, more productive habit patterns.

As more people in your organization begin to implement these improved work habits, they'll be more likely to feel fulfilled and happy staying with you. This is the ultimate "win-win-win" situation. Each employee wins, their manager wins, and the whole organization wins. Fostering personal growth is one of the easiest and most rewarding ways to enjoy quantum gains in productivity for any organization, not to mention making everyone's job far less stressful and a lot more fun.

The End

Me, Myself & the Author

I began my working life as a paper boy at age 13. I got a busboy job at 16 and worked for eight years in the restaurant business as a waiter in several Scottsdale, Arizona restaurants to pay my way through school.

Upon graduating from Arizona State University in 1980 with an Industrial Engineering degree, I worked for two years in a large manufacturing company. Then, I spent two years with a small family owned manufacturing business before starting my own recognition award, incentive and gift business, Recognition Concepts, Inc.

While I can't speak for everyone just entering the workforce, for me, fresh out of college, employment was a real eye-opener. I was prepared from a knowledge basis, and knew how to gather and process information. What took me by surprise, though, as I began my career in a turbine engine manufacturing facility, was the vast range of competency I saw among people who were supposedly at the same job levels, and the time-wasting survival habits of people who had been there longer than I.

What I had expected to be a group of inspired, like-minded professionals turned out to be a stress-filled pecking order with a disproportionate amount of time being spent covering up weaknesses, or perceived weaknesses, in every department. I had just completed college, graduating with an Industrial Engineering degree, and found myself working alongside people with the same title and job description as mine, but who had previously worked as a drill press operator. It was a shock, and immediately put a lot of strain on these new relationships. I was the new guy with the fancy degree and that made these other guys nervous. It wasn't my fault, but there was always an underlying need for the old timers to show me what they could do and, by inference, what I couldn't.

On the shop floor, I got a quick lesson on how the machine operators could manipulate the process engineers into believing a certain machining operation took far longer than it really did. They thought managers were there to make them work harder, even though our job was actually to determine the true cost of making engine components. I got smart pretty quick, and figured out a way of talking to an operator about his job while I was actually timing the guy on the next machine. That way, I could see what was really going into each operation.

I saw people jealously hoard work space and office furniture that were not necessary to their job function. I saw numbers manipulated to make programs look more complete, or performances more successful, than they really were. None of these actions individually would constitute criminal fraud, insubordination, or necessarily lead to catastrophic engine failures, yet it amazed me how much time and energy was wasted covering up inefficiencies rather than addressing them. Actively cooperating with whomever or whatever was required to improve quality (especially when the solutions seemed pretty obvious to me) sure appeared to be a superior option. I came to realize that our universities do a great job of imparting book knowledge, but a poor one of preparing us to get along with other people, work as teams, and overcome the inherent politics that come with competitive work situations.

After more than 15 years of working with major

corporations to improve their employee recognition, motivation and incentive programs, I've seen a lot when it comes to what makes employees tick. With knowledge and understanding, employees and employers can work together to optimize the employment experience.

Most of all, I believe that all people have the capacity to become far more than they think they can be, and that the resources required are freely available, if they simply choose to make use of them.

The *Ten Levels of Workplace Disillusionment* may be a humorous take on things, but I hope it helps you take a serious look at the problem of low employee morale that still plagues so many companies in our country today. Many of the causes – and some of the solutions – for these destructive job-related characteristics are provided in this book, *The Vocational Shrink – An Analysis of the Ten Levels of Workplace Disillusionment*.

There's much more to be said and discussed, because morale is an ongoing issue, and I hope I'll have the chance to meet with you face-to-face at a future seminar or workshop. By now you can tell how much I enjoy working with clients to offer management training and recognition programs . . . and to help organizations like yours maximize their greatest resource – People!

About the Illustrator

Brian Freeman attended Phoenix Institute of Technology where he studied Architectural Illustration. He soon realized that his aptitude for drawing and painting people exceeded his knowledge of architecture.

He found work as a mural painter and illustrator in Tempe, Arizona where he eventually met John Schaefer. That meeting turned into a lasting friendship with John, who has utilized Brian's design and illustration talents on a number of corporate montage projects for the PaintMyStory® division of Recognition Concepts, Inc.

By the way, what started as a doodled caricature of John on the margin of a preliminary layout turned into the basis of many "Vocational Shrink" illustrations found in this book. "I have always loved the little caricature that Brian did of me," says John. "I framed it and it has hung over my desk for the past ten years, reminding me, in a humorous way, to never give up or take myself too seriously. When I realized that some fun illustrations would be perfect to personalize this book, the choice was immediate and obvious. Brian's cartoons always make me laugh!"

Brian works as a fine artist in several mediums, and teaches drawing and painting with pastels. He lives with his wife Pam in Tucson, Arizona with their two dogs and cat.

An Analysis of the Ten Levels of
Workplace Disillusionment

Appendix 1
The Vocational Shrink – The Game

The purpose of *the Vocational Shrink – The Game*, is to help make people aware of the negative habit patterns they utilize in their workplace, counterproductive habits that allow them to slip back into various deep-seated and inefficient states. Our game depicting *"Ten Levels of Workplace Disillusionment"* seems to work best with groups of people who are equally willing to step back and look at themselves from a distance, be open-minded, and realize that true success in life starts when a person takes charge of his or her own actions.

Used as part of a training regimen in a workplace setting the game can lead to shared fun, effortless education, and hopefully growing morale among all who participate. Management support and acknowledgement of the values this exercise represents will allow your company to make the best use of *The Vocational Shrink* game and other materials at a departmental level or companywide.

Level 2's will fight it, Level 4's will misunderstand it, Level 6's will make fun of it, Level 9's will be scared of it but, overall, most people will find our game to be a fun and ultimately valuable tool that helps put a finger on the core of many of their personal issues, as well as a number of the organization's problems. If it yields a happy, more productive workforce, management will love it.

Having worked in a number of jobs prior to starting my own business, I can honestly say that it sure would have been nice to have a game as a proactive morale training resource back then. From all accounts, though, life in the workforce hasn't changed all that much in the past 15 years.

Remember that the awareness generated by our book *The Vocational Shrink – An Analysis of The Ten Levels of Workplace Disillusionment* is for personal growth of the participants, not to be used judgmentally or negatively. The security created by a group of under-standing friends (even the Level 6's can be serious from time to time) is paramount in supporting a person as they modify their behavior. Greater confidence and im-proved self-esteem will begin to permeate the workplace as employees become aware of, and deal with, negative habits, idiosyncrasies, and subconscious reaction pat-terns. Abraham Maslow, the famous psychologist, said it this way, "If you plan on being anything less than you are capable of being, you will probably be unhappy all the days of your life."

If you experience particularly meaningful transfor-mations or improvements in your organization, please let me know by e-mailing me at john@vocationalshrink. com. I would like to share your success and feedback with other customers, which will enhance their experi-ence with the program.

Now, let the Games begin!

Appendix 2
My Spiritual Journey

I had several brushes with a personal God experience during college, but until my friend shared his version of God as a real, down-to-earth, personal, and readily available partner, who really knew and cared about me, I was a spiritual loner. Think about it a minute. Unless you are an atheist, and can logically justify in your mind that all life as we know it is a total coincidence, you have to believe there is a higher power of some kind out there. Somebody figured out how to make plants give off oxygen and the animals breathe it in. Somebody developed a cooling system for our planet where winds blow across the ice at the top and bottom, and keep all the temperatures around the world in ranges that allow us to stay alive. Somebody created a brain that can allow us to create the technology and lifestyle that we all enjoy from a sphere of dirt, chemicals, water and plants. Little did I know that this same awesome power built me, knew me, cared about me, and was available to help me through life.

Here's what my friend told me. Get a Bible and read what God has to say. Simple, huh? Get a New American Standard, New International Version, or even a Living Bible – these are the easiest to read. Go to the New Testament and read the first four chapters, Matthew, Mark, Luke, John. I read the book of John first, but I don't think it really matters the order you use. Before you read, decide if you believe that The Bible is actually the inspired word of God. If you do, then ask God to interpret His words for you and show you how He wants you to handle this mess you call life. If you don't believe that, then pray for Him to show you it is. If you are a real ultra left-brainer who wants concrete proof, then get a copy of Josh McDowell's book, *Evidence That Demands a Verdict,* but do that after you read the four gospels.

Again, if you're anything like me, kind of proud, feeling rather silly about the idea of reading a 2,000 year-old book where some ghost is going to share with you the secret of life – that's good! Then you may get the same message I did. Few ever actually got to see God in the Old Testament of the Bible. Jesus came to Earth in the form of a man so we could see what He was talking about and showed us a very simple plan for man's life. All He asks us to do is:

• Repent of our sins – That's Bible talk for admitting that you screwed up here and there while trying to figure out life on your own.

• Be baptized – All that means is a public expression of your commitment to Him in front of other people. Hey, this guy is busy and he wants to know that you are at least serious enough about giving him a shot at helping you, and that you do more than just whisper your intentions to yourself under your breath.

• Get out of His way – Give Him a chance to make your life all He planned for it to be.

Easier said than done because, as soon is it starts to look a little nicer, we have the tendency to grab it back and tell him we have the idea. Commit to giving Him control for the long haul and avoid the propensity to grab it out of His hands before He's through. Sound simple enough? It has to be! Imagine if you were God, and you needed to put a plan together to help a bunch of folks like you and me – it better be pretty simple, right? The problem is, we are those same people I talked about earlier who have a lifetime of deeply seated habits regarding how we need to take care of ourselves. Most find the idea of submission to be harder than rolling up their sleeves.

My book is almost over, so finish it first, before you grab your Bible. If you have read any other books about how to make the most of your life, you have heard this same kind of advice in one form or another. Zig Ziglar is pretty open about what God did to change his perspective rather late in life. Scott Alexander, in his excellent

Rhinoceros Success[3] books, recommends that we become rhinos to succeed in the jungle of life and that God is available as your safari guide.

If we didn't all struggle to figure out how to best live our lives, books like mine and all the others wouldn't exist, so at least give it the benefit of the doubt that there may be a better alternative than just trying harder using the limited knowledge and skills you have. You are willing to take automotive advice from your mechanic, golf advice from the club pro, fishing advice from the local expert angler, and computer advice from your PC manufacturer. Why not let the guy who designed and built you have a little say in how to operate and maintain the machine you live in?

Notice that I am not saying run over and immediately join your neighborhood church, give them all your money, join the choir, and volunteer for every ministry that you can find. Not to say that God won't necessarily lead you to a good church and people who will help you grow in your understanding of how The Lord works. But this is not the first step. The most important thing is to begin reading God's book. Each time before you read, ask Him to explain it to you, and then just take it as it comes. Don't have expectations or set limits, just read and share your desires. Then look out, because you may just begin to get what you asked of Him.

Now don't get all hung up on that fancy praying stuff like you've seen on TV or heard on the radio. Praying is just you talking with God. He already knows all about you – He just wants to hear you say it. So just talk, then listen. As you read, you will do more listening than talking and will begin to slowly understand the nature of God. He's a pretty nice guy, loves you very much, has incredible patience, and a great sense of humor. If you let Him, God's

---

[3] Rhinoceros Success books, by Scott Alexander. Rhino Press. 800-872-3274

Spirit will move into a place in your heart that He has had set aside all along, and amazing things will begin to happen.

God is like a blacksmith. He forms us with fire and hammer blows. You may not like the heat or the hits, but when you look back at the results, you will see that your hard head may have needed a whack now and then to get you where He wanted you to be. With this in mind, be careful what you pray for, because if you get it, you'll get the path leading to it first. I prayed for a more humble, loving and patient personality. God blessed me with a family and several business opportunities. As I grow in my ability to understand, appreciate, and bene-fit from these responsibilities, the humility, patience and loving personality I sought are slowly developing in my life. Like happiness, you may pray for it, but it actually comes as a by-product of improving your way of living. God offers the path, but you choose to take it and learn from the experiences.

The same goes for financial prayers. The Bible says ". . . my cup runneth over" (Psalms 23:5 KJV). It also says " . . . whatever you ask for in prayer, believe that you have received it, and it will be yours" (Mark 11:24NIV). While each of these thoughts are used in a different context, they both assume motive. If your motives are not right, it won't happen, or your motives will have to be reshaped, which can take some painful lessons. God is that good friend who will do anything for you, but won't beat around the bush with you either.

If you take me up on my recommendation and just commit to giving an honest read of His first four books in the New Testament, you can then make your decision to read on and accept the help of this new, personal best friend. It won't immediately make your life easier. As a matter of fact, it will probably make life harder, because He will lead you to evaluate and confront many of your current activities, friends, work habits, and life motives. But if you allow Him to work with you long enough, you will truly become all you can imagine and much more.

All of the practice you get identifying and changing

the habits in your life will make you better and better at the process of personal change overall. You will become an expert habit modifier, and will develop greater confidence, so you can take on bigger, tougher habits as time goes on. In the workplace, you'll move toward becoming the best manager or staffer you can be. With God's help, I have become mentally stronger, more efficient in everything I do, more balanced in all areas of life, and able to make much more sacrificial, considerate decisions. I am a lot less selfish and have made it a habit to forgo the "now" for a better "later" in many areas of life where I used to think I "needed" or "deserved" certain things.

Best of all, God can use all of us little people in small ways to make big differences in other peoples lives, if we let Him. As you begin to give off that special aura of love, faith and contentment (a by-product of God's Spirit living in your heart), you too will be given opportunities to share this way of looking at life. No pressure, no handing out pamphlets at the airport, no street corner preaching – just letting the way you live and the intensity of your beliefs rub off on others as they go by. There is no better feeling in our world.

I hope you will take this invitation to start this process and use all the resources available to you in order to begin the journey to where you want to be. If you can recognize or relate to any of the *Ten Levels* in this book, you are already poised to climb out from behind the limitations that got you there and you're about to begin a growth phase that will do nothing short of astound you. The best part will be when you begin to see the cumulative effects of all the people who get picked up in your wake as you revitalize your life and begin to see all that you can be and do. I hope you will share your journey with me and with others, as that is what God's plan is all about.

I am happy to share my experiences, opinions and success with regard to my spiritual journey with individuals and companies who wish to integrate this message into their workplace. Please feel free to email me at john@VocationalShrink.com.

How to Order

To order additional copies of
The Vocational Shrink –
An Analysis of The Ten Levels
of Workplace Disillusionment

- Visit www.VocationalShrink.com
- Call (888) 646-6670
- Fax us a photocopy of the **ORDER FORM**
    to (623) 572-1333
- Or just mail a photocopy of the **ORDER FORM**
    with your check or credit card
    information to:

Schaefer Recognition & Media Group, LLC
7131 W. Planada Lane
Glendale, AZ 85310

- International Orders please call us for
    detailed pricing and shipping information
    at (888) 646-6670

Schaefer Recognition & Media Group, LLC
is a division of Recognition Concepts, Inc.

U.S. ORDER FORM

Order using this form, or our web site www.VocationalShrink.com

☐ The Vocational Shrink – **The Book** ___ x 16.95 = _____

☐ The Vocational Shrink – **The Game** ___ x 19.95 = _____

    U.S. Shipping / Handling (1st book/game/set) =   6.00

    (each additional book/game/set) ___ x 2.00 = _____

International and 6+ quantity shipping costs; please call or email us.

    Sales Tax (Arizona residents add 8.1%) _____

                    Total Enclosed _____

☐ Sign me up for The Vocational Shrink – **The Newsletter**.

☐ Let me know about bulk pricing on The Vocational Shrink – **The Book** and The Vocational Shrink – **The Game**.

☐ Contact me about The Vocational Shrink – **The Seminar** for motivating my managers and employees.

please print

SHIPPING / BILLING

Name _____

Company _____

Title _____

Address _____

City, State, Zip _____

Phone _____ Email_____

PAYMENT

☐ Check # _____   ☐ AMERICAN EXPRESS   ☐ MasterCard   ☐ VISA®

Credit Card Number _____

ExpirationDate_(xx/xxxx)_____ 3DigitAuthorizationCode_____

Schaefer Recognition & Media Group, LLC

Schaefer Recognition & Media Group, LLC
7131 W. Planada Lane, Glendale, AZ 85310
(888)646-6670   www.VocationalShrink.com